Fodor's
New *FIFTH EDITION*

Caribbean
Ports of Call

Portions of this book appear in *Fodor's Caribbean*

Fodor's Travel Publications, Inc.
New York • Toronto • London • Sydney • Auckland
www.fodors.com

Fodor's Caribbean Ports of Call

EDITORS: Stephanie Adler, Laura M. Kidder

Editorial Contributors: Carol Bareuther, John Bigley, Carla Armour, David H. Jones, Lynda Lohr, Karl Luntta, Paris Permenter, Heidi Sarna, M. T. Schwartzman, Jordan Simon, Simon Worrall, Jane Zarem

Editorial Production: Linda K. Schmidt

Maps: David Lindroth, *cartographer*; Robert Blake, *map editor*

Design: Fabrizio La Rocca, *creative director*; Jolie Novak, *photo editor*

Production/Manufacturing: Mike Costa

Cover Photograph: Catherine Karnow (bottom photo), Norwegian Cruise Line (top photo)

Cover Design: Allison Saltzman

Copyright

Fifth Edition

ISBN 0–679–00347–9

ISSN 1090–7343

Special Sales

PRINTED IN THE UNITED STATES OF AMERICA

10 9 8 7 6 5 4 3 2 1

CONTENTS

Maps

Don't Forget to Write

Keeping a travel guide fresh and up-to-date is a big job. So we love your feedback—positive and negative—and follow up on all suggestions. Contact the *Caribbean Ports of Call* editor at editors@fodors.com or c/o Fodor's, 201 East 50th Street, New York, New York 10022. And have a wonderful trip!

Important Tip

Although all prices, opening times, and other details in this book are based on information supplied to us at press time, changes occur all the time in the travel world, and Fodor's cannot accept responsibility for facts that become outdated or for inadvertent errors or omissions. So **always confirm information when it matters,** especially if you're making a detour to visit a specific place.

Karen Cure
Editorial Director

1 Cruise Primer

BEFORE YOU GO

Tickets, Vouchers, and Other Travel Documents

After you make the final payment to your travel agent, the cruise line will issue your cruise tickets and vouchers for airport–ship transfers. Depending on the airline, and whether you have purchased an air-sea package, you may receive your plane tickets or charter-flight vouchers at the same time; you may also receive vouchers for any shore excursions, although most cruise lines issue these aboard ship. Should your travel documents not arrive when promised, contact your travel agent or cruise line. If you book late, tickets may be delivered directly to the ship.

Passports and Visas

Carrying a passport is always a good idea, and entry requirements do change, so read your cruise documents carefully to see what you'll need for embarkation. (You don't want to be turned away at the pier!)

In the past, cruise lines sailing from Florida ports to the Caribbean rarely asked to see passports from American passengers. This has changed, and it's now advisable to be prepared to show your passport. If you don't, you may be asked to fill out a citizenship form—delaying your embarkation.

If you are boarding a ship outside the United States, you'll need the appropriate entry requirements for that country. On cruises to or from some countries, you may be required to obtain a visa in advance. Check with your travel agent or cruise line about specific requirements. If you do need a visa for your cruise, your travel agent should help you obtain it, through a visa service by mail or directly from the consulate or embassy. (There may be a charge of up to $25 for this service, added to the visa charge.)

What to Pack

Certain packing rules apply to all cruises: Always take along a sweater in case of cool evening ocean breezes or overactive air-conditioning. A rain slicker usually comes in handy, too, and make sure you take at least one pair of comfortable walking shoes for exploring port towns. Men should pack a dark suit, a tuxedo, or a white dinner jacket. Women should pack one long gown or cocktail dress for every two or three formal evenings on board.

Generally speaking, plan on one outfit for every two days of cruising, especially if your wardrobe contains many interchangeable pieces. Ships often have convenient laundry facilities as well. And don't overload your luggage with extra toiletries and sundry items; they are easily available in port and in the ship's gift shop (though usually at a premium price). Soaps, and sometimes shampoos and body lotion, are often placed in your cabin by the cruise line.

Outlets in cabin bathrooms are usually compatible with U.S.-purchased appliances. This may not be the case on older ships or those with European registries; call ahead if this is a concern for you. Most cabin bathrooms are equipped with low-voltage outlets for electric shavers, and many newer ships have built-in hair dryers.

Take an extra pair of eyeglasses or contact lenses in your carry-on luggage. If you have a health problem that requires a prescription drug, pack enough to last the duration of the trip or have your doctor write a prescription using the drug's generic name, because brand names vary from country to country. Always carry prescription drugs in their original packaging to avoid problems with customs officials. Don't pack them in luggage that you plan to check, in case your bags go astray. Pack a list of the offices that supply refunds for lost or stolen traveler's checks.

Although no two cruises are quite the same, evening dress tends to fall into three categories.

FORMAL
Formal cruises celebrate the ceremony of cruising. Jackets and ties for men are the rule for dinner, tuxedos are not uncommon, and the dress code is observed faithfully throughout the evening.

SEMIFORMAL
Semiformal cruises are a bit more relaxed than their formal counterparts. Men wear a jacket and tie most nights.

CASUAL

Casual cruises are the most popular. Shipboard dress and lifestyle are informal. Men dress in sport shirts and slacks for dinner most nights, in jackets and ties only two or three evenings of a typical seven-day sailing.

ARRIVING AND DEPARTING

If you have purchased an air-sea package, you will be met by a cruise-company representative when your plane lands at the port city and then shuttled directly to the ship in buses or minivans. Some cruise lines arrange to transport your luggage between airport and ship—you don't have to hassle with baggage claim at the start of your cruise or with baggage check-in at the end. If you decide not to buy the air-sea package but still plan to fly, ask your travel agent if you can use the ship's transfer bus anyway. Otherwise, you will have to take a taxi to the ship.

If you live close to the port of embarkation, bus transportation may be available. If you are part of a group that has booked a cruise together, this transportation may be part of your package. Another option for those who live close to their point of departure is to drive to the ship. The major U.S. cruise ports all have parking facilities.

Embarkation

Check-In

On arrival at the dock, you must check in before boarding your ship. (A handful of smaller cruise ships handle check-in at the airport.) An officer will collect or stamp your ticket, inspect or even retain your passport or other official identification, ask you to fill out a tourist card, check that you have the correct visas, and collect any unpaid port or departure tax. Seating assignments for the dining room are often handed out at this time, too. You may also register your credit card to open a shipboard account, although that may be done later at the purser's office.

After this you may be required to go through a security check and to pass your hand baggage through an X-ray inspection. These are the same machines in use at airports, so ask to have your photographic film inspected by hand.

Although it takes only five or ten minutes per family to check in, lines are often long, so aim for off-peak hours. The worst time tends to be immediately after the ship begins boarding; the later it is, the less crowded. For example, if boarding is from 2 PM to 4:30, try to arrive after 3:30.

Boarding the Ship

Before you walk up the gangway, the ship's photographer will probably take your picture; there's no charge unless you buy the picture (usually $6). On board, stewards may serve welcome drinks in souvenir glasses—for which you're usually charged between $3 and $5 in cash.

You will either be escorted to your cabin by a steward or, on a smaller ship, given your key by a ship's officer and directed to your cabin. Some elevators are unavailable to passengers during boarding, since they are used to transport luggage. You may arrive to find your luggage outside your stateroom or just inside the door; if it hasn't arrived a half hour before sailing, contact the purser. If you are among the unlucky few whose luggage doesn't make it to the ship in time, the purser will have it flown to the next port.

Visitors' Passes

Some cruise ships permit passengers to invite guests on board prior to sailing, although most cruise lines prohibit all but paying passengers from boarding for reasons of security and insurance liability. Cruise companies that allow visitors usually require that you obtain passes several weeks in advance; call the lines for policies and procedures.

Most ships do not allow visitors while the ship is docked in a port of call. If you meet a friend on shore, you won't be able to invite him or her back to your stateroom.

Disembarkation

The last night of your cruise is full of business. On most ships you must place everything except your hand luggage outside your door, ready to be picked up by midnight. Color-coded tags, distributed to your cabin in a debarkation packet, should be placed on your luggage before the crew collects it. Your color will determine when you leave the ship and help you retrieve your luggage on the pier.

Your shipboard bill is left in your room during the last day; to pay the bill (if you haven't already put it on your credit card) or to settle any questions, you must stand in line at the purser's office. Tips to the cabin steward and dining staff are distributed on the last night.

The next morning, in-room breakfast service is usually not available because stewards are too busy. Most passengers clear out of their cabins as soon as possible, gather their hand luggage, and stake out a chair in one of the public lounges to await the ship's clearance through customs. Be patient—it takes a long time to unload and sort thousands of pieces of luggage. Passengers are disembarked in groups according to the color-coded luggage tags; those with the earliest flights get off first. If you have a tight connection, notify the purser before the last day, and he or she may be able to arrange faster preclearing and debarkation.

Customs and Duties

U.S. Customs

Before your ship lands, each individual or family must fill out a customs declaration, regardless of whether anything was purchased abroad. If you have less than $1,400 worth of goods, you will not need to itemize purchases. Be prepared to pay whatever duties are owed directly to the customs inspector, with cash or check.

U.S. Customs now preclears a number of ships sailing in and out of Miami and other ports—it's done on the ship before you disembark. In other ports you must collect your luggage from the dock, then stand in line to pass through the inspection point. This can take up to an hour.

Allowances. You may bring home $400 worth of foreign goods duty-free if you've been out of the country for at least 48 hours and haven't already used the $400 exemption, or any part of it, in the past 30 days. Note that these are the *general* rules, applicable to most countries; passengers on certain Caribbean or Panama Canal itineraries may be entitled to bring back $600 worth of goods duty free, and if you're returning from a cruise that called in the U.S. Virgin Islands, the duty-free allowance is higher—$1,200.

Alcohol and Tobacco. Travelers 21 or older may bring back 1 liter of alcohol duty-free, provided the beverage laws of the state through which they reenter the United States allow it. If they have visited the U.S. Virgin Islands, 5 liters are allowed. In addition, 100 non-Cuban cigars and 200 cigarettes are allowed, regardless of your age. From the U.S. Virgin Islands, 1,000 cigarettes are allowed, but only 200 of them may have been acquired elsewhere. Antiques and works of art more than 100 years old are duty-free.

U.S. CUSTOMS FOR FOREIGNERS

If you hold a foreign passport and will be returning home within hours of docking, you may be exempt from all U.S. Customs duties. Everything you bring into the United States must leave with you when you return home. When you reach your own country, you will have to pay duties there.

Canadian Customs

Allowances. If you've been out of Canada for at least seven days, you may bring in C$500 worth of goods duty-free. If you've been away less than seven days but more than 48 hours, the duty-free exemption drops to C$200. You cannot pool exemptions with family members. Goods claimed under the C$500 exemption may follow you by mail; those claimed under the lesser exemption must accompany you.

Alcohol and Tobacco. Alcohol and tobacco products may be included in the seven-day and 48-hour exemption. If you meet the age requirements of the province or territory through which you reenter Canada, you may bring in, duty-free, 1.14 liters (40 imperial ounces) of wine or liquor *or* two dozen 12-ounce cans or bottles of beer or ale. If you are 16 or older, you may bring in, duty-free, 200 cigarettes, 50 cigars or cigarillos, and 400 tobacco sticks or 400 grams of manufactured tobacco. Alcohol and tobacco must accompany you on your return.

ON BOARD

Checking Out Your Cabin

The first thing to do upon arriving at your cabin or suite is to make sure that everything is in order. If there are two twin beds instead of the double bed you wanted, or other problems, ask to be moved *before* the ship departs. Unless the ship is full, you can usually persuade the chief house-keeper or hotel manager to allow you to change cabins. It is customary to tip the stewards who help you move.

Since your cabin is your home away from home for a few days or weeks, everything should be to your satisfaction. Take a good look around: Is the cabin clean and orderly? Do the toilet, shower, and faucets work? Check the tele-phone and television. Again, major problems should be ad-dressed immediately. Minor concerns, such as a shortage of pillows, can wait until the frenzy of embarkation sub-sides.

Your dining-time and seating-assignment card may be in your cabin; now is the time to check it and immediately re-quest any changes. The maître d' usually sets up shop in one of the public rooms specifically for this purpose.

Shipboard Accounts

Virtually all cruise ships operate as cashless societies. Pas-sengers charge onboard purchases and settle their ac-counts at the end of the cruise with a credit card, traveler's checks, or cash. You can sign for wine at dinner, drinks at the bar, shore excursions, gifts in the shop—virtually any expense you may incur aboard ship. On some lines, an imprint from a major credit card is necessary to open an account. Otherwise, a cash deposit may be required and a positive balance maintained to keep the shipboard account open. Either way, you will want to open a line of credit soon after settling in if an account was not opened for you at embarkation. This can easily be arranged by visiting the purser's office, in the central atrium or main lobby.

Tipping

For better or worse, tipping is an integral part of the cruise experience. Most companies pay their cruise staff nominal wages and expect tips to make up the difference. Most cruise lines have recommended tipping guidelines, and on many ships "voluntary" tipping for beverage service has been replaced with a mandatory 15% service charge, which is added to every bar bill. On the other hand, the most expensive luxury lines include tipping in the cruise fare and may prohibit crew members from accepting any additional gratuities. On most small adventure ships, a collection box is placed in the dining room or lounge on the last full day of the cruise, and passengers contribute anonymously.

Dining

Ocean liners serve food nearly around the clock. There may be up to four breakfast options: early-morning coffee and pastries on deck, breakfast in bed through room service, buffet-style in the cafeteria, and sit-down in the dining room. There may also be several lunch choices, mid-afternoon hors d'oeuvres, and midnight buffets. You can eat whatever is on the menu, in any quantity, at as many of these meals as you wish. Room service is traditionally, but not always, free (*see* Shipboard Services, *below*).

Restaurants

The chief meals of the day are served in the main dining room, which on most ships can accommodate only half the passengers at once. Meals are therefore usually served in two sittings—early (or main) and late (or second) seatings. Early seating for dinner is generally between 6 and 6:30, late seating between 8 and 8:30.

Most cruise ships have a cafeteria-style restaurant, usually near the swimming pool, where you can eat lunch and breakfast (dinner is usually served only in the dining room). Many ships provide self-serve coffee or tea in their cafeteria around the clock, as well as buffets at midnight.

Increasingly, ships also have alternative restaurants for ethnic cuisines, such as Italian, Chinese, or Japanese food. These are found mostly on newer vessels, although some older liners have been refitted for alternative dining. Other ships have pizzerias, ice-cream parlors, and caviar or cappuccino bars; there may be an extra charge at these facilities.

More and more lines are banning smoking in their main dining rooms. Smoking policies vary; contact your cruise line to find out what the situation will be on your cruise.

Seatings

When it comes to your dining-table assignment, you should have options on four important points: early or late seating; smoking or no-smoking section (if smoking is allowed in the dining room); a table for two, four, six, or eight; and special dietary needs. When you receive your cruise documents, you will usually receive a card asking for your dining preferences. Fill this out and return it to the cruise line, but remember that you will not get your seating assignment until you board the ship. Check it out immediately, and if your request was not met, see the maître d'—usually there is a time and place set up for changes in dining assignments.

On some ships, seating times are strictly observed. Ten to 15 minutes after the scheduled mealtime, the dining-room doors are closed. On other ships, passengers may enter the dining room at their leisure, but they must be out by the end of the seating. When a ship has just one seating, passengers may enter at any time while the kitchen is open.

Seating assignments on some ships apply only for dinner. Several have open seating for breakfast or lunch, which means you may sit anywhere at any time. Smaller or more luxurious ships offer open seating for all meals.

CHANGING TABLES

Dining is a focal point of the cruise experience, and your companions at meals may become your best friends on the cruise. However, if you don't enjoy the company at your table, the maître d' can usually move you to another one if the dining room isn't completely full—a tip helps. He will probably be reluctant to comply with your request after the first full day at sea, however, because the waiters, busboys, and wine steward who have been serving you up to that point won't receive their tips at the end of the cruise. Be persistent if you are truly unhappy.

Cuisine

Most ships serve food geared to the American palate, but there are also theme dinners featuring the cuisine of a particular country. Some European ships, especially smaller vessels, may offer a particular cuisine throughout the cruise—Scandinavian, German, Italian, or Greek, perhaps—depending on the ship's or the crew's nationality. Aboard all cruise ships, the quality of the cooking is generally good, but even a skilled chef is hard put to serve 500 or more extraordinary dinners per hour. But the presentation is often spectacular, especially at gala midnight buffets.

There is a direct relationship between the cost of a cruise and the quality of its cuisine. The food is very sophisticated on some (mostly expensive) lines, among them Crystal Cruises, Cunard Line, Seabourn Cruise Line, and Silversea Cruises. In the more moderate price range, Celebrity Cruises has gained renown for the culinary stylings of French chef Michel Roux, who acts as a consultant to the line.

Special Diets

With notification well in advance, many ships can provide a kosher, low-salt, low-cholesterol, sugar-free, vegetarian, or other special menu. However, there's always a chance that the wrong dish will somehow be handed to you. Especially when it comes to soups and desserts, it's a good idea to ask about the ingredients.

Large ships usually offer an alternative "light" or "spa" menu based upon American Heart Association guidelines, using less fat, leaner cuts of meat, low-cholesterol or low-sodium preparations, smaller portions, salads, fresh-fruit desserts, and healthy garnishes. Some smaller ships may not be able to accommodate special dietary needs. Vegetarians generally have no trouble finding appropriate selections.

Wine

Wine at meals costs extra on most ships; the prices are usually comparable to those in shoreside restaurants and are charged to your shipboard account. A handful of luxury vessels include both wine and liquor.

The Captain's Table

It is both a privilege and a marvelous experience to be invited to dine one evening at the captain's table. Although some seats are given to celebrities, repeat passengers, and passengers in the most expensive suites, other invitations are given at random to ordinary passengers. You can request an invitation from the chief steward or the hotel manager, although there is no guarantee you will be accommodated. The captain's guests always wear a suit and tie or a dress, even if the dress code for that evening is casual. On many ships, passengers may also be invited to dine at the other officers' special tables, or officers may visit a different passenger table each evening.

Bars

A ship's bars, whether adjacent to the pool or attached to one of the lounges, tend to be its social centers. Except on a handful of luxury-class ships where everything is included in the ticket price, bars operate on a pay-as-it's-poured basis. Rather than demand cash after every round, however, most ships allow you to charge drinks to an account.

In international waters there are, technically, no laws against teenage drinking, but almost all ships require passengers to be over 18 or 21 to purchase alcoholic drinks. Many cruise ships have chapters of Alcoholics Anonymous (a.k.a. "Friends of Bill W.") or will organize meetings on request. Look for meeting times and places in the daily program slipped under your cabin door each night.

Entertainment

Lounges and Nightclubs

On ocean liners, the main entertainment lounge or showroom schedules nightly musical revues, magic acts, comedy performances, and variety shows. During the rest of the day the room is used for group activities, such as shore-excursion talks or bingo games. Generally, the larger the ship, the bigger and more impressive the productions. Newer ships have elaborate showrooms that often span two decks. Some are designed like an amphitheater while others have two levels—a main floor and a balcony. Seating is sometimes in clusters of armchairs set around cocktail tables. Other ships have more traditional theater-style seating.

Many larger ships have a second showroom. Entertainment and ballroom dancing may go on here late into the night. Elsewhere you may find a disco, nightclub, or cabaret, usually built around a bar and dance floor. Music is provided by a piano player, a disc jockey, or by performing ensembles such as country-and-western duos or jazz combos.

On smaller ships the entertainment options are more limited, sometimes consisting of no more than a piano around which passengers gather. There may be a main lounge where scaled-down revues are staged.

Library

Most cruise ships have a library with up to 1,500 volumes, from the latest best-sellers to reference works. Many shipboard libraries also stock videotapes.

Movie Theaters

All but the smallest vessels have a room for screening movies. On older ships and some newer ones, this is often a genuine cinema-style movie theater. On other ships, it may be just a multipurpose room. The films are frequently one or two months past their first release date but not yet available on videotape or cable TV. Films rated "R" are edited to minimize sex and violence. On a weeklong voyage, a dozen different films may be screened, each one repeated at various times during the day. Theaters are also used for lectures, religious services, and private meetings.

With a few exceptions, ocean liners equip their cabins with closed-circuit TVs; these show movies (continuously on some newer ships), shipboard lectures, and regular programs (thanks to satellite reception). Ships with VCRs in the cabins usually provide a selection of movies on cassette at no charge (a deposit is sometimes required).

Casinos

Once a ship is 12 mi off American shores, it is in international waters and gambling is permitted. (Some "cruises to nowhere," in fact, are little more than sailing casinos.) All ocean liners, as well as many cruise yachts and motor-sailing ships, have casinos. On larger vessels, they usually have poker, baccarat, blackjack, roulette, craps, and slot machines. House stakes are much more modest than those in Las Vegas or Atlantic City. On most ships the maximum bet is $200;

some ships allow $500. Payouts on the slot machines (some of which take as little as a nickel) are generally much lower, too. Credit is never extended, but many casinos have handy credit-card machines that dispense cash for a hefty fee.

Children are officially barred from the casinos, but it's common to see them playing the slots rather than the adjacent video machines. Most ships offer free individual instruction and even gambling classes in the off-hours. Casinos are usually open from early morning to late night, although you may find only unattended slot machines before evening. In adherence to local laws, casinos are always closed while a ship is in port.

Game Rooms
Most ships have a game or card room with card tables and board games. These rooms are for serious players and are often the site of friendly round-robin competitions and tournaments. Most ships furnish everything for free (cards, chips, games, and so forth), but a few charge $1 or more for each deck of cards. Be aware that professional cardsharps and hustlers have been fleecing ship passengers almost as long as there have been ships. There are small video arcades on most medium and large ships. Family-oriented ships often have a computer learning center as well.

Bingo and Other Games
The daily high-stakes bingo games are even more popular than the casinos. You can play for as little as a dollar a card. Most ships have a snowball bingo game with a jackpot that grows throughout the cruise into hundreds or even thousands of dollars. Another popular cruise pastime is the so-called "horse races": Fictional horses are auctioned off to "owners." Individual passengers can buy a horse or form "syndicates." Bids usually begin at around $25 and can top $1,000 per horse. Races are then "run" according to dice throws or computer-generated random numbers. Audience members bet on their favorites.

Sports and Fitness

Swimming Pools
All but the smallest ships have at least one pool, some of them elaborate affairs with water slides or retractable roofs;

hot tubs and whirlpools are quite common. Pools may be filled with fresh water or salt water; some ships have one of each. While in port or during rough weather, the pools are usually emptied or covered with canvas. Many are too narrow or too short to allow swimmers more than a few strokes in any direction; none have diving boards, and not all are heated. Often there are no lifeguards. Wading pools are sometimes provided for small children.

Sun Deck

The top deck is usually called the Sun Deck or Sports Deck. On some ships this is where you'll find the pool or whirlpool; on others it is dedicated to volleyball, table tennis, shuffleboard, and other such sports. A number of ships have paddle-tennis courts, and a few have golf driving ranges. Often, after the sun goes down, the Sun Deck is used for dancing, barbecues, or other social activities.

Exercise and Fitness Rooms

Most newer ships and some older ones have well-equipped fitness centers, many with massage, sauna, and whirlpools. An upper-deck fitness center often has an airy and sunny view of the sea; an inside, lower-deck health club is often dark and small unless it is equipped with an indoor pool or beauty salon. Many ships have full-service exercise rooms with bodybuilding and cardiovascular equipment, aerobics classes, and personal fitness instruction. Some ships even have cruise-length physical-fitness programs, which may include lectures on weight loss or nutrition. These often are tied in with a spa menu in the dining room. Beauty salons adjacent to the health club may offer spa treatments such as facials and mud wraps. The more extensive programs are often sold on a daily or weekly basis.

Promenade Deck

Many vessels designate certain decks for fitness walks and may post the number of laps per mile. Fitness instructors may lead daily walks around the Promenade Deck. A number of ships discourage jogging and running on the decks or ask that no one take fitness walks before 8 AM or after 10 PM, so as not to disturb passengers in cabins. With the advent of the megaship, walking and jogging have in many cases moved up top to tracks on the Sun or Sports deck.

Shipboard Services

Room Service

A small number of ships have no room service at all, except when the ship's doctor orders it for an ailing passenger. Many offer only breakfast (Continental on some, full on others), while others provide no more than a limited menu at certain hours of the day. Most, however, have selections that you can order at any time. Some luxury ships have unlimited round-the-clock room service. There usually is no charge other than for beer, wine, or spirits.

Minibars

An increasing number of ships equip their more expensive cabins with small refrigerators or minibars stocked with snacks, soda, and liquors, which may or may not be free.

Laundry and Dry Cleaning

All but the smallest ships and shortest cruises offer laundry services—full-service, self-service, or both. Use of machines is generally free, although some ships charge for detergent, use of the machines, or both. Valet laundry service includes cabin pickup and delivery and usually takes 24 hours. Most ships also offer dry-cleaning services.

Hair Stylists

Even the smallest ships have a hair stylist on staff. Larger ships have complete beauty salons, and some have barbershops. Book your appointment well in advance, especially before such popular events as the farewell dinner.

Film Processing

Many ships have color-film processing equipment to develop film overnight. It's expensive but convenient.

Photographer

The staff photographer, a near-universal fixture on cruise ships, records every memorable, photogenic moment. The thousands of photos snapped over the course of a cruise are displayed publicly in special cases every morning and are offered for sale, usually for $6 for a 5″ × 7″ color print or $12 for an 8″ × 10″. If you want a special photo or a portrait, the photographer is usually happy to oblige. Many passengers choose to have a formal portrait taken before the captain's farewell dinner—the dressiest evening of the cruise. The ship's photographer usually anticipates this demand by setting up a studio near the dining-room entrance.

Religious Services

Most ships provide nondenominational religious services on Sundays and religious holidays, and a number offer Catholic masses daily and Jewish services on Friday evenings. The kind of service held depends upon the clergy the cruise line invites on board. Usually religious services are held in the library, the theater, or one of the private lounges, although a few ships have actual chapels.

Communications

SHIPBOARD

Most cabins have loudspeakers and telephones. Generally, the loudspeakers cannot be switched off because they are needed to broadcast important notices. Telephones are used to call fellow passengers, order room service, summon a doctor, request a wake-up call, or speak with any of the ship's officers or departments.

SHIP TO SHORE

Satellite facilities make it possible to call anywhere in the world from most ships. Most are also equipped with telex and fax machines, and some provide credit card–operated phones. It may take as long as a half hour to make a connection, but unless a storm is raging outside, conversation is clear and easy. On older ships, voice calls must be put through on shortwave wireless or via the one phone in the radio room. Newer ships are generally equipped with direct-dial phones in every cabin for calls to shore. Be warned: the cost of sending any message, regardless of the method, can be quite expensive—up to $15 a minute. (On some ships, though, it's much cheaper, costing as little as $3.95 a minute.) If possible, wait until you go ashore to call home.

Safety at Sea

Fire Safety

The greatest danger facing cruise-ship passengers is fire. All of the lines reviewed in this book must meet certain international standards for fire safety. The latest rules require that ships have sprinkler systems, smoke detectors, and other safety features. However, these rules are designed to protect against loss of life. They do not guarantee that a fire will not happen; in fact, fire is relatively common on cruise ships. The point here is not to alarm, but to emphasize the importance of taking fire safety seriously.

Fire safety begins with you, the passenger. Once settled into your cabin, find the location of your life vests and review the emergency instructions inside the cabin door or near the life vests. Make sure your vests are in good condition and learn to secure them properly. Make certain the ship's purser knows if you have some physical infirmity that may hamper a speedy exit from your cabin. In case of a real emergency, the purser can quickly dispatch a crew member to assist you. If you are traveling with children, be sure that child-size life jackets are placed in your cabin.

Within 24 hours of embarkation, you will be asked to attend a mandatory lifeboat drill. Do so and listen carefully. If you are unsure of how to use your vest, now is the time to ask. Only in the most extreme circumstances will you need to abandon ship—but it has happened. The time you spend learning the procedure may serve you well in a mishap.

Health Care

Quality medical care at sea is another important safety issue. All big ships are equipped with medical infirmaries to handle minor emergencies. However, these should not be confused with hospitals. There are no international standards governing medical facilities or personnel aboard cruise ships, although the American Medical Association has recommended that such standards be adopted. If you have a preexisting medical condition, discuss your upcoming cruise with your doctor. Pack an extra supply of any medicines you might need. Once aboard, see the ship's doctor and alert him or her to your condition, and discuss treatments or emergency procedures before any problem arises. Passengers with potentially life-threatening conditions should seriously consider signing up with a medical evacuation service, and all passengers should review their health insurance to make sure they are covered while on a cruise.

If you become seriously ill or injured and happen to be near a modern major city, you may be taken to a medical facility shoreside. But if you're farther afield, you may have to be airlifted off the ship by helicopter and flown either to the nearest American territory or to an airport where you can be taken by charter jet to the United States. Many standard health insurance policies, as well as Medicare, do not cover these or other medical expenses incurred outside the United States. You can, however, buy supplemental health insurance to cover you while you're traveling.

The most common minor medical problems confronting cruise passengers are seasickness and gastrointestinal distress. Modern cruise ships, unlike their transatlantic prede-cessors, are relatively motion-free vessels with computer-controlled stabilizers, and they usually sail in relatively calm waters. If, however, you do feel queasy, you can always get seasickness pills aboard ship. (Many ships give them out for free at the front desk.)

Outbreaks of food poisoning happen from time to time aboard cruise ships. Episodes are random; they can occur on ships old and new, big and small, budget and luxury. The Centers for Disease Control and Prevention (CDC) mon-itors cruise-ship hygiene and sanitation procedures, con-ducting voluntary inspections twice a year of all ships that sail regularly from U.S. ports (this program does not include ships that never visit the United States). For a free listing of the latest ship scores, write the CDC's National Center for Environmental Health (Vessel Sanitation Program, 1015 North America Way, Room 107, Miami, FL 33132). You can also get a copy from the CDC's fax-back service at 888/232–3299. Request publication 510051. Another alternative is to visit the Centers' Web site at www.cdc.gov.

A high score on the CDC report doesn't mean you won't get sick. Outbreaks have taken place on ships that consis-tently score very highly; conversely, some ships score very poorly yet passengers never get sick.

Crime on Ships
Crime aboard cruise ships has become headline news, thanks in large part to a few well-publicized cases. Most people never have any type of problem, but you should ex-ercise the same precautions aboard ship that you would at home. Keep your valuables out of sight—on big ships vir-

tually every cabin has a small safe in the closet. Don't carry too much cash ashore, use your credit card whenever possible, and keep your money in a secure place, such as a front pocket that's harder to pick. Single women traveling with friends should stick together, especially when returning to their cabins late at night. And be careful about whom you befriend, as you would anywhere, whether it's a fellow passenger or a member of the crew. Don't be paranoid, but do be prudent.

GOING ASHORE

Traveling by cruise ship presents an opportunity to visit many places in a short time. The flip side is that your stay in each port of call will be limited. For this reason, cruise lines offer shore excursions, which maximize passengers' time by organizing tours for them. There are a number of advantages to shore excursions: In some destinations, transportation may be unreliable, and a ship-packaged tour is the best way to see distant sights. Also, you don't have to worry about missing the ship. The disadvantage of a shore excursion is the cost—you pay more for the convenience of having the ship do the legwork for you. Of course, you can always book a tour independently, hire a taxi, or use foot power to explore on your own.

Arriving in Port

When your ship arrives in a port, it will tie up alongside a dock or anchor out in a harbor. If the ship is docked, passengers walk down the gangway to go ashore. Docking makes it easy to move between the shore and the ship.

Tendering

If your ship anchors in the harbor, however, you will have to take a small boat—called a launch or tender—to get ashore. Tendering is a nuisance. When your ship first arrives in port, everyone wants to go ashore. Often, in order to avoid a stampede at the tenders, you must gather in a public room, get a boarding pass, and wait until your number is called. This continues until everybody has disembarked. Even then, it may take 15–20 minutes to get ashore if your ship is anchored far offshore. Because tenders can be difficult to board, passengers with mobility problems may not be able to visit certain ports. The larger the ship, the more likely it will use tenders. It is usually possible to learn before booking a cruise whether the ship will dock or anchor at its ports of call. (For more information about where ships dock, tender, or both at each port, *see* Chapter 2.)

Before anyone is allowed to walk down the gangway or board a tender, the ship must be cleared for landing. Immigration and customs officials board the vessel to examine passports and sort through red tape. It may be more than an hour before you're allowed ashore. You will be issued a boarding pass, which you'll need to get back on board.

Returning to the Ship

Cruise lines are strict about sailing times, which are posted at the gangway and elsewhere and announced in the daily schedule of activities. Be certain to be back on board at least a half hour before the announced sailing time or you may be stranded. If you are on a shore excursion that was sold by the cruise line, however, the captain will wait for your group before casting off. That is one reason many passengers prefer ship-packaged tours.

If you're not on one of the ship's tours and the ship sails without you, immediately contact the cruise line's port representative, whose phone number is often listed on the daily schedule of activities. You may be able to hitch a ride on a pilot boat, though that is unlikely. Passengers who miss the boat must pay their own way to the next port.

2 Ports of Call

CRUISING THE CARIBBEAN

Nowhere in the world are conditions better suited to cruising than in the Caribbean Sea. Tiny island nations, within easy sailing distance of one another, form a chain of tropical enchantment that curves from Cuba in the north all the way down to the coast of Venezuela. There's far more to life here than sand and coconuts, however. The islands are vastly different, with their own cultures, topographies, and languages. Colonialism has left its mark, and the presence of the Spanish, French, Dutch, Danish, and British is still felt. Slavery, too, has left its cultural legacy, blending African overtones into the colonial/Indian amalgam. The one constant, however, is the weather. Despite the islands' southerly latitude, the climate is surprisingly gentle, due in large part to the cooling influence of the trade winds.

The Caribbean is made up of the Greater Antilles and the Lesser Antilles. The former consists of those islands closest to the United States: Cuba, Jamaica, Hispaniola (Haiti and the Dominican Republic), and Puerto Rico. (The Cayman Islands lie south of Cuba.) The Lesser Antilles, including the Virgin, Windward, and Leeward islands and others, are greater in number but smaller in size, and constitute the southern half of the Caribbean chain.

More cruise ships ply these waters than any others in the world. There are big ships and small ships, fancy ships and party ships. In peak season, it's not uncommon for thousands of passengers to disembark from several ships into a small town on the same day—a phenomenon not always enjoyed by locals. With such an abundance of cruise ships in this area, however, you can choose an itinerary that suits you best. Cruises of the western Caribbean often include port calls in Key West and Cozumel. Eastern Caribbean itineraries usually stop at Nassau in the Bahamas.

When to Go

Average year-round temperatures throughout the Caribbean are 78°F–85°F, with a low of 65°F and a high of 95°F; downtown shopping areas always seem to be unbearably hot. High season runs from December 15 to April 14. During this most fashionable, most expensive, and most crowded time to go, reservations up to a year in advance are necessary for many

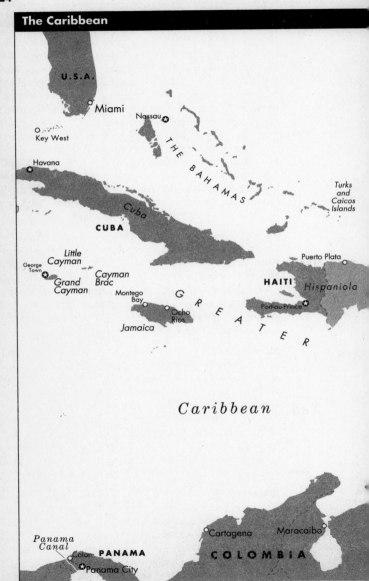

U.S.A.

Miami

Key West

Nassau

THE BAHAMAS

Havana

Turks and Caicos Islands

Cuba

CUBA

Puerto Plata

Little Cayman

George Town

Cayman Brac

Grand Cayman

Montego Bay

G R E A T E R

HAITI

Hispaniola

Port-au-Prince

Ocho Rios

Jamaica

Caribbean

Cartagena

Maracaibo

Panama Canal

Colon

PANAMA

Panama City

COLOMBIA

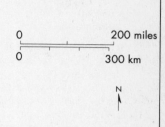

0   200 miles

0   300 km

N

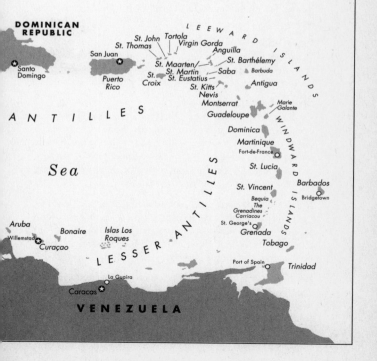

ATLANTIC OCEAN

DOMINICAN REPUBLIC

LEEWARD ISLANDS

St. John   Tortola
St. Thomas   Virgin Gorda
San Juan   Anguilla
    St. Maarten/   St. Barthélemy
Santo   St. Martin   Saba   *Barbuda*
Domingo   St.   St. Eustatius
   Puerto   Croix   St. Kitts   *Antigua*
   Rico   Nevis
      Montserrat   Marie
A N T I L L E S   Guadeloupe   *Galante*

W I N D W A R D   I S L A N D S

Dominica

Martinique
Fort-de-France

Sea   *St. Lucia*

St. Vincent   *Barbados*
   Bequia   Bridgetown
   The
   Grenadines
Aruba   Carriacou
Willemstad   *Bonaire*   *Islas Los*   St. George's
  Curaçao   *Roques*   *Grenada*
       L E S S E R   A N T I L L E S   *Tobago*

Port of Spain   *Trinidad*

La Guaira

Caracas

V E N E Z U E L A

ships. A low-season (summer) visit offers certain advantages: Temperatures are virtually the same as in winter (even cooler on average than in parts of the U.S. mainland), island flora is at its height, and the water is smoother and clearer. Some tourist facilities close down in summer, however, and many ships move to Europe, Alaska, or the northeastern United States.

Hurricane season runs from June 1 through November 30. Although cruise ships stay well out of the way of these storms, hurricanes and tropical storms—their less-powerful relatives—can affect the weather throughout the Caribbean for days, and damage to ports can force last-minute itinerary changes.

Currency

Currencies vary throughout the islands, but U.S. dollars and credit cards are widely accepted. Don't bother changing more than a few dollars into local currency for phone calls, tips, and taxis.

Passports and Visas

American citizens boarding ships in the United States usually need neither a passport nor visas to call at Caribbean ports. However, carrying a passport is always a good idea.

Shore Excursions

Typical excursions include a bus tour of the island or town, a visit to a local beach or rum factory, boat trips, snorkeling or diving, and charter fishing. It's always safest to take a ship-arranged excursion, but it's almost never cheapest. You also sacrifice the freedom to explore at your own pace and the joys of venturing off the beaten path.

If you seek adventure, find a knowledgeable taxi driver or tour operator—they're usually within a stone's throw of the pier—and wander around on your own. A group of four to six people will find this option more economical and practical than will a single person or a couple.

Renting a car is also a good option on many islands—again, the more people, the better the deal. But get a good island map before you set off, and be sure to find out how long it will take you to get around.

Conditions are ideal for water sports of all kinds—scuba diving, snorkeling, windsurfing, sailing, waterskiing, and fishing excursions abound. Your shore-excursion director can usually arrange these activities for you individually if the ship offers no formal excursion.

Dining

Cuisine on the Caribbean's islands is hard to classify. The region's history as a colonial battleground and ethnic melting pot creates plenty of variety. The one quality that defines most Caribbean cooking is its essential spiciness. Dress is generally casual, though throughout the islands beachwear is often inappropriate.

CATEGORY	COST*
$$$	over $30
$$	$15–$30
$	under $15

per person for a three-course meal, excluding drinks, service, and sales tax

Antigua

Some say Antigua has so many beaches that you could visit a different one every day for a year. Most have snow-white sand, and many are backed by lavish resorts that offer sailing, diving, windsurfing, and snorkeling.

The larger of the British Leeward Islands, Antigua was the headquarters from which Lord Horatio Nelson (then a mere captain) made his forays against the French and pirates in the late 18th century. A decidedly British atmosphere still prevails, underscored by a collection of pubs that will raise the spirits of every Anglophile. If you have a taste for history you'll want to explore English Harbour and its carefully restored Nelson's Dockyard, as well as tour old forts, historic churches, and tiny villages. If you like to hike, you can wander through a tropical rain forest lush with pineapples, bananas, and mangoes. If you have an interest in archaeology you can head for the megaliths of Greencastle and explore excavations of ancient Indian sites.

About 4,000 years ago Antigua was home to a people called the Ciboney. They disappeared mysteriously, and the island remained uninhabited for about 1,000 years. When Columbus sighted the 173-square-km (108-square-mi) island in 1493, the Arawaks had already set up housekeeping. The English moved in 130 years later, in 1623. Then a sequence of bloody battles involving the Caribs, the Dutch, the French, and the English began. Africans had been captured as slaves to work the sugar plantations by the time the French ceded the island to the English in 1667. On November 1, 1981, Antigua, with Barbuda, its sister island 48 km (30 mi) to the north, achieved full independence. The combined population of the two islands is about 70,000—only 1,200 of whom live on Barbuda.

Currency

Antigua uses the Eastern Caribbean (E.C.) dollar, commonly known as beewees. Figure about EC$2.70 to US$1. Although U.S. dollars are generally accepted, you may get your change in beewees. All prices given below are in U.S. dollars unless otherwise indicated.

Telephones

Calling the United States is a simple matter of dialing 1 to reach AT&T's USADirect.

Shore Excursions

The following are good choices in Antigua. They may not be offered by all cruise lines. Times and prices are approximate.

ISLAND SIGHTS

Nelson's Dockyard and Countryside. Get a sense of Antigua's British Colonial history with great views along the way. The highlight is a visit to Nelson's Dockyard, a gem of Georgian British maritime architecture and a must for history buffs and Anglophiles. *3 hrs. Cost: $35.*

If you want to feel like Indiana Jones, opt for a tour with **Tropikelly** (tel. 809/461–0383). You'll be given an insider's look via four-wheel drive at the whole island, complete with deserted plantation houses, rain-forest trails, ruined sugar mills and forts, and even a picnic lunch with drinks. The highlight is the luxuriant tropical forest around the island's highest point, Boggy Peak. *5 hrs. Cost: $65.*

Coming Ashore

Though some ships dock at the deep-water harbor in downtown St. John's, most use the town's Heritage Quay, a multimillion-dollar complex with shops, condominiums, a casino, and a food court. Most St. John's attractions are an easy walk from Heritage Quay; the older part of the city is eight blocks away. A tourist information booth is in the main docking building.

If you intend to explore beyond St. John's, consider hiring a taxi driver-guide. Taxis meet every cruise ship. They're unmetered; fares are fixed, and drivers are required to carry a rate card. Agree on the fare before setting off, and plan to tip drivers 10%.

Exploring Antigua

Numbers in the margin correspond to points of interest on the Antigua map.

① St. John's is home to about 40,000 people (more than half the island's population). The city has seen better days, but there are some notable sights. At the far south end of town, where Market Street forks into Valley and All Saints roads, locals jam the marketplace every Friday and Saturday to buy and sell fruits, vegetables, fish, and spices. Be sure to ask before you aim a camera, and expect the subject of your shot to ask for a tip.

If you have a serious interest in archaeology, see the historical displays at the **Museum of Antigua and Barbuda.** The colonial building that houses the museum is the former courthouse, which dates from 1750. *Church and Market Sts., tel. 268/462–1469. Admission: $2 suggested donation. Open weekdays 8:30–4, Sat. 10–1.*

Two blocks east of the Museum of Antigua and Barbuda on Church Street is the Anglican **St. John's Cathedral,** which sits on a hilltop, surrounded by its churchyard. At the south gate are figures said to have been taken from one of Napoléon's ships. A previous structure on this site was destroyed by an earthquake in 1843, so the interior of the current church is completely encased in pitch pine to forestall heavy damage from future quakes. *Between Long and Newcastle Sts., tel. 268/461–0082. Admission free.*

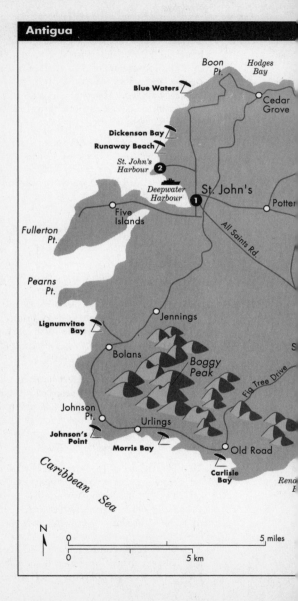

Antigua

Boon
Pt.

Hodges
Bay

Blue Waters

Cedar
Grove

Dickenson Bay

Runaway Beach

*St. John's
Harbour*

2

*Deepwater
Harbour*

St. John's

1

Potter

Five
Islands

All Saints Rd.

*Fullerton
Pt.*

*Pearns
Pt.*

Jennings

**Lignumvitae
Bay**

Bolans

*Boggy
Peak*

Fig Tree Drive

Johnson
Pt.

Urlings

**Johnson's
Point**

Morris Bay

Old Road

**Carlisle
Bay**

*Reno
E*

Caribbean Sea

N

| 0 | | 5 miles |
| 0 | | 5 km |

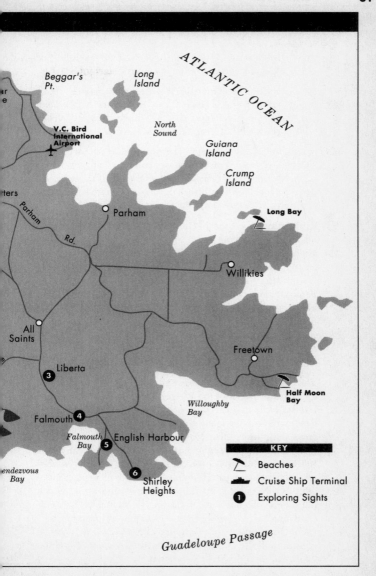

ATLANTIC OCEAN

Beggar's Pt.

Long Island

V.C. Bird International Airport

North Sound

Guiana Island

Crump Island

Parham Rd.

Parham

Long Bay

Willikies

All Saints

Freetown

Liberta

Half Moon Bay

Willoughby Bay

Falmouth

Falmouth Bay

English Harbour

Shirley Heights

Rendezvous Bay

KEY

Beaches

Cruise Ship Terminal

Exploring Sights

Guadeloupe Passage

A favorite car excursion is to follow Fort Road northwest out of town. After 3 km (2 mi) you'll come to the ruins of **② Ft. James,** named for King James II. If you continue on this road, you'll arrive at Dickenson Bay, with its string of smart, expensive resorts on one of many beautiful beaches.

In the opposite direction from St. John's, 13 km (8 mi) south **③** on All Saints Road is **Liberta,** one of the first settlements founded by freed slaves. East of the village, on Monk's Hill, are the ruins of Ft. George, built in 1669.

④ Falmouth, 2¼ km (1½ mi) farther south, sits on a lovely bay, backed by former sugar plantations and sugar mills. St. Paul's Church, dating from the late 18th and early 19th centuries, held services for the military in Nelson's time. It has been restored and is now used for Sunday worship.

⑤ English Harbour, the most famous of Antigua's attractions, lies on the coast just south of Falmouth. The Royal Navy abandoned the station in 1889, but it has been restored as Nelson's Dockyard, which epitomizes the colonial Caribbean. Within the compound are crafts shops, hotels, a marina, and restaurants. The Admiral's House Museum has rooms displaying ship models, a model of English Harbour, and artifacts from Nelson's days. The museum lost several artifacts to Hurricane Georges in 1998 and was nearly totalled; it was on the mend at press time. *Tel. 268/463–1053. Admission: $2. Open daily 8–6.*

The English Harbor area has a number of other attractions. On a ridge overlooking Nelson's Dockyard is Clarence House, built in 1787 and once the home of the duke of Clarence. As you leave the dockyard, turn right at the crossroads in English Harbour and drive up to Shirley **⑥** Heights for a spectacular harbor view. Nearby, the **Dows Hill Interpretation Center** chronicles the island's history and culture from Amerindian times to the present. A high-light of the center is its multimedia presentation in which illuminated displays, incorporating lifelike figures and colorful tableaux, are presented with running commentary, television, and music—resulting in a cheery, if bland, portrait of Antiguan life. *National Parks Authority, tel. 268/460–1053. Admission: EC$15. Open daily 9–5.*

Shopping

Redcliffe Quay and Heritage Quay are waterfront markets with boutiques, restaurants, and snack bars. The main tourist shops in St. John's are along St. Mary's, High, and Long streets. In general, shops are open Monday–Saturday 8:30–noon and 1–4; some shops close for the day at noon on Thursday and Saturday. The duty-free shops of Heritage Quay often have more flexible hours. Redcliffe Quay, a collection of 19th-century buildings painted in cotton-candy colors, contains more unique boutiques.

At Redcliffe Quay, try **Jacaranda** (tel. 268/462–1888) for batiks, sarongs, and swimwear. **Base** (tel. 268/460–2500) is where you'll find striped and monochrome cotton-and-Lycra resort wear from English designer Steven Giles; his creations are all the rage on the island. At the **Goldsmitty** (tel. 268/462–4601), Hans Smit turns gold and precious and semiprecious stones into one-of-a-kind works of art. **Noreen Phillips** (tel. 268/462–3127) creates glitzy appliqued and beaded evening wear inspired by the colors of the sea and sunset. **Kate Designs** (tel. 268/460–5971) sells acclaimed artist Kate Spencer's flowing painted silk scarves and sarongs, as well as vividly colored prints, place mats, and note cards. Across the street, down a narrow alley in a charming 19th-century gingerbread house, **Coates Cottage** (tel. 268/462–0179) sells some of the highest-quality local artwork at the lowest prices—a bonus is that artists and artisans often use the space as a temporary studio.

In downtown St. John's, the **Map Shop** (St. John's St., tel. 268/462–3993) has a wonderful collection of antique maps and nautical books and charts. **CoCo Shop** (St. Mary's St., tel. 268/462–1128) sells Sea Island cotton designs, Daks clothing, and Liberty of London fabrics.

At Heritage Quay, **La Casa Habana** (tel. 268/462–2677) has Cuban cigars (though these cannot be legally brought back with you into the United States). You'll also find a wide range of duty-free shops and factory-outlet stores, from **Body Shop** and **Benetton** to **Polo** and **Gucci.**

Sports

GOLF

You'll find an 18-hole course at **Cedar Valley Golf Club** (tel. 268/462–0161).

SCUBA DIVING

Antigua has plenty of wrecks, reefs, and marine life. **Dockyard Divers** (St. John's, tel. 268/464–8591), run by British ex–merchant seaman Captain A. G. Finchman, is one of the oldest and most reputable diving and snorkeling outfits on the island.

Beaches

Antigua's 366 beaches are public, and many are dotted with resorts that provide water-sports equipment rentals and a place to grab a cool drink. Since most hotels have taxi stands, you can get back to the ship easily. The following are just a few excellent possibilities: **Carlisle Bay,** where the Atlantic meets the Caribbean Sea, is a long, snow-white beach with the Curtain Bluff resort as a backdrop. A large coconut grove adds to its tropical beauty. **Dickenson Bay** has a lengthy stretch of powder-soft white sand and a host of hotels that cater to water-sports enthusiasts. **Half Moon Bay,** a 1½-km (¾-mi) crescent of shell-pink sand, is another great place for snorkeling and windsurfing. **Johnson's Point** is a deliciously deserted beach of bleached white sand on the southwest coast.

Dining

In restaurants a 10% service charge and 7% tax are usually added to the bill.

$$ **Admiral's Inn.** Known simply as "the Ads" to yachtsmen around the world, this historic inn in the heart of English Harbour is a must for Anglophiles and mariners. Dine on velvety pumpkin soup, fresh snapper with lime, or lobster thermidor while taking in the splendid harbor views. *Nelson's Dockyard, tel. 268/460–1027. Reservations essential. AE, MC, V.*

$$ **Redcliffe Tavern.** Set amid the courtyards of Redcliffe Quay, on the second floor of a colonial warehouse, this appealing restaurant has an inventive menu that's part northern Italian, part Continental, part Creole, and all fresh. Antique water-pumping equipment, salvaged from all over the island, adds to the unusual dining experience. *Redcliffe Quay, St. John's, tel. 268/461–4557. AE, MC, V.*

Aruba

Though the "A" in the ABC (Aruba, Bonaire, Curaçao) Islands is small—only 31 km (19 mi) long and 10 km (6 mi) at its widest—the island's national anthem proclaims "the greatness of our people is their great cordiality," and this is no exaggeration. Once a member of the Netherlands Antilles, Aruba became independent within the Netherlands in 1986, with its own royally appointed governor, a democratic government, and a 21-member elected parliament. Long secure in a solid economy—with good education, housing, and health care—the island's population of nearly 89,000 treats visitors as welcome guests. English is spoken everywhere.

The island's distinctive beauty lies in the stark contrast between the sea and the countryside: rocky deserts, cactus jungles, secluded coves, and aquamarine panoramas with crashing waves. It's famous mostly, however, for its duty-free shops, the glorious 11.3-km (7-mi) strand of Palm and Eagle Beaches, and casinos.

Currency
Arubans accept U.S. dollars, so you need only exchange a little money for pocket change. Local currency is the Aruban florin (AFl). At press time, the exchange rate was AFl1.77 to US$1. Note that the Netherlands Antilles florin used in Bonaire and Curaçao is not accepted on Aruba. All prices given below are in U.S. dollars unless otherwise indicated.

Telephones
Local calls from a pay phone cost AFl1.25. International calls can be placed at the phone center in the cruise-ship terminal. To reach the United States, dial 001, the area code, and the local number.

Shore Excursions
The following are good choices on Aruba. They may not be offered by all cruise lines. Times and prices are approximate.

Aruba Town and Countryside Drive. A comprehensive town-and-country bus tour takes in the major island sights, including the breathtaking limestone Natural Bridge; the California Lighthouse, set amid vanilla sand dunes; the desolate Alto Vista Chapel; boulder formations that resemble abstract sculptures; and various caves stippled with petroglyphs and filled with stalactites and stalagmites. After the tour, passengers may stay in town, on the beach, or at the casino. *3 hrs. Cost: $28.*

***Atlantis* Submarine.** Aboard a 65-ft submarine, passengers dive 50–90 ft below the surface along Aruba's Barcadera Reef. *2 hrs. Cost: $72.*

Glass-Bottom Boat Tour. The view of undersea creatures is less dramatic than aboard the *Atlantis* submarine, but the price is less expensive, too. *2 hrs. Cost: $40.*

Coming Ashore

Ships tie up at the Aruba Port Authority cruise terminal; inside are a tourist information booth and duty-free shops. From here, you're a five-minute walk from various shopping districts and downtown Oranjestad. Just turn right out of the cruise-terminal entrance.

The "real" Aruba—what's left of its wild, untamed beauty—can only be experienced on a drive through the countryside (though be aware that, except for those in a few restaurants, there are no public bathrooms). Since car rental agencies are slow and roads aren't always clearly marked, your best bet is to hire a taxi (you can flag one in the street). Rates are fixed, so confirm the fare before setting off. It should cost about $25 an hour for up to four people.

Exploring Aruba

Numbers in the margin correspond to points of interest on the Aruba map.

❶ Aruba's charming capital, **Oranjestad,** is best explored on foot. If you're interested in Dutch architecture, begin at the corner of Oude School Straat and walk three blocks toward the harbor to Wilhelminastraat, where some of the buildings date from Oranjestad's 1790 founding. Walk west and you'll pass old homes, a government building, and the Protestant church. When you reach Shuttestraat again, turn left and go one block to Zoutmanstraat.

The small **Archaeology Museum** in Oranjestad has two rooms of Indian artifacts, farm and domestic utensils, and skeletons. *J. E. Irausquinplein 2A, tel. 297/8–28979. Admission free. Open weekdays 8–noon and 1–4.*

Ft. Zoutman, the island's oldest building, was built in 1796 and used as a fortress in skirmishes between British and Curaçao troops. The Willem III Tower was added in 1868. The museum displays island relics in an 18th-century Aruban house. *Zoutmanstraat, tel. 297/8–26099. Admission: $1.15. Open weekdays 9–noon and 1:30–4:30.*

Just behind the St. Francis Roman Catholic Church is the **Numismatic Museum,** displaying money from more than 100 countries. *Zuidstraat 7, tel. 297/8–28831. Admission free. Open weekdays 7:30–noon and 1–4:30.*

2 The 541-ft **Hooiberg** (Haystack Hill) is midisland; you can climb 562 steps to the top for an impressive view. To get there from Oranjestad, turn onto Caya G. F. Croes (shown on island maps as 7A) toward Santa Cruz; the peak will be on your right.

For a shimmering panorama of blue-green sea, drive east on L. G. Smith Boulevard toward San Nicolas. Turn left where you see the drive-in theater. At the first intersection, turn right, **3** then follow the curve to the right to **Frenchman's Pass,** a dark, luscious stretch of highway arbored by overhanging trees. Legend claims the French and native Indians warred here during the 17th century for control of the island.

Near Frenchman's Pass are the cement and limestone ruins **4** of the **Balashi Gold Smelter** (follow the directions to Frenchman's Pass, *above,* and then take the dirt road veering to the right), a lovely place to picnic, listen to the parakeets, and contemplate the towering cacti. A gnarled divi-divi tree stands at the entrance.

5 The area called **Spanish Lagoon** is where pirates once hid to repair their ships (follow L. G. Smith Boulevard, which crosses straight over the lagoon). It's a picturesque place for a picnic or to enjoy the island scenery.

38

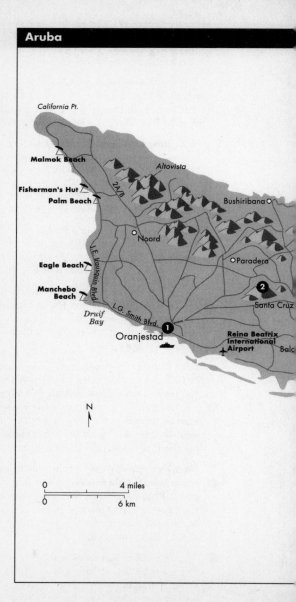

Aruba

California Pt.

Malmok Beach

Altovista

2A/B

Fisherman's Hut
Palm Beach

Bushiribana O

O Noord

Eagle Beach

O Paradera

Manchebo Beach

L.E. Jausquin Blvd.

L.G. Smith Blvd.

Santa Cruz

Druif Bay

Oranjestad

Reina Beatrix International Airport

Bala

N

0   4 miles

0   6 km

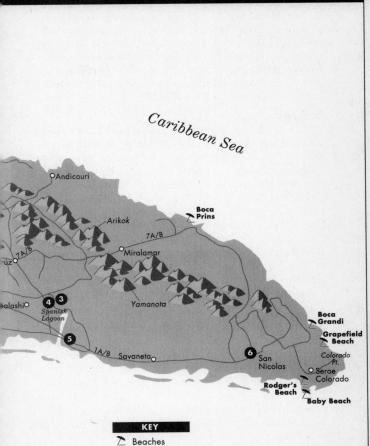

Caribbean Sea

Andicouri

Arikok

Boca
Prins

7A/B

Miralamar

úz○

7A/B

alashi○

4 **3**

Spanish
Lagoon

Yamanota

5

1A/B   Savaneta○

Boca
Grandi

Grapefield
Beach

Colorado
Pt.

6 San
Nicolas

○Seroe
Colorado

Rodger's
Beach

Baby Beach

KEY

⩔ Beaches

⛴ Cruise Ship Terminal

1 Exploring Sights

⑥ San Nicolas is Aruba's oldest village. In the 1980s, the town, with its oil refinery, was a bustling port with a rough-and-tumble quality; now it's dedicated to tourism, with the Main Street promenade full of interesting kiosks. Charlie's Bar (Zeppenfeldstraat 56) on the main street is a popular tourist lunch spot. While you eat your "jumbo and dumbo" shrimp, you can gawk at the thousands of license plates, old credit cards, baseball pennants, and hard hats covering every inch of the walls and ceiling.

Shopping

Caya G. F. Betico Croes in Oranjestad is Aruba's chief shopping street. Several malls—gabled, pastel-hued re-creations of traditional Dutch colonial architecture—house branches of such top names as Tommy Hilfiger, Little Switzerland, Nautica, and Benetton; the ritziest are the Royal Plaza and Seaport Village Malls, both right near the cruise-ship pier. The stores are full of Dutch porcelains and figurines, as befits the island's Netherlands heritage. Also consider the Dutch cheeses (you're allowed to bring up to 1 pound of hard cheese through U.S. Customs), hand-embroidered linens, and any product made from the native aloe vera plant. There's no sales tax, and Arubans consider it rude to haggle.

Artesania Aruba (L. G. Smith Blvd. 178, tel. 297/8–37494) has home-crafted pottery and folk objets d'art. **Aruba Trading Company** (Caya G. F. Betico Croes 12, tel. 297/8–22602) discounts brand-name perfumes and cosmetics (first floor), and jewelry and men's and women's clothes (second floor) up to 30%. **Gandelman Jewelers** (Caya G. F. Betico Croes 5–A, tel. 297/8–34433) sells jewelry as well as a full line of watches. **Wulfsen & Wulfsen** (Caya G. F. Betico Croes 52, tel. 297/8–23823) is one of Holland's best stores for fine-quality clothes and shoes.

Sports

FISHING

Contact **De Palm Tours** in Oranjestad (tel. 297/8–24400 or 800/766–6016) for information on fishing charters.

GOLF

The **Aruba Golf Club** near San Nicolas (tel. 297/8–42006) has a 9-hole course with 20 sand and 5 water traps, roaming goats, and lots of cacti. Greens fees are $10 for nine holes, $18 for 18. Caddies and rental clubs are available. The Robert Trent Jones–designed, 18-hole, par-71 course, **Tierra del Sol** (Malmokweg, tel. 297/8–67800), sits on the northwest coast near the California Lighthouse. It combines Aruba's native beauty—the flora and rock formations—with the lush greens of the world's best courses. The $120 greens fee includes a golf cart. Club rentals are $25–$45.

HIKING

De Palm Tours (tel. 297/8–24400 or 800/766–6016) offers a guided three-hour trip to remote sites of unusual natural beauty that are accessible only on foot. The fee is $25 per person, including refreshments and transportation; a minimum of four people is required.

HORSEBACK RIDING

Rancho El Paso (tel. 297/8–73310) offers one-hour jaunts ($20) that take you through countryside dotted with cacti, divi-divi trees, and aloe vera plants; two-hour trips ($40) go to the beach as well. Wear lots of sunblock.

WATER SPORTS

De Palm Tours (tel. 297/8–24400 or 800/766–6016) has a near monopoly on water sports, including equipment and instruction for scuba diving, snorkeling, and windsurfing. However, **Pelican Watersports** (tel. 297/8–72302 or 297/8–31228) and **Red Sail Sports** (tel. 297/8–61603) may offer cheaper rates for snorkeling, sailing, windsurfing, and scuba-diving packages.

Beaches

Beaches in Aruba are beautiful and clean. On the north side the water is too choppy for swimming, but the views are great. **Palm Beach**—which stretches behind the Americana, Aruba Palm Beach, Holiday Inn, Hyatt, Radisson, and Wyndham hotels—is the center of Aruban tourism, offering the best in swimming, sailing, and fishing. In high season, however, it's packed, and you might prefer the adjoining **Eagle Beach,** which is anchored by the minivillage of La Cabana Suite Resort and is even closer to town. **Manchebo Beach,** by the Bucuti Beach Resort, is an impressively wide stretch of white powder. You'll see "topfree" bathers here from time to time. On the island's eastern tip, tiny **Baby**

Beach is as placid as a wading pool and only 4 or 5 ft deep—perfect for tots and bad swimmers. Thatched shaded areas provide relief from the sun.

Dining

Restaurants usually add a 10%–15% service charge.

$$$ **Chez Mathilde.** This elegant restaurant occupies one of the last surviving 19th-century houses on the island. Dine either in the light-filled greenhouse atrium or a more intimate, swooningly romantic, antiques-filled room. The French-style menu is continually being re-created. Feast on the likes of artfully presented baked escargots with herbs and garlic, braised monkfish in watercress and vermouth sauce, or filet mignon in a signature pepper sauce prepared table-side. Then, too, there are crêpes suzettes and profiteroles to tempt the taste buds. *Havenstraat 23, Oranjestad, tel. 297/8–34968. Reservations essential. AE, MC, V. No lunch Sun.*

$–$$ **Boonoonoonoos.** The name—say it just as it looks!—means extraordinary, which is a bit of hyperbole for this Austrian-owned Caribbean bistro in the heart of town. The specialty here is Pan-Caribbean cuisine: the roast chicken Barbados is sweet and tangy, marinated in piña colada sauce. The Jamaican jerk ribs (a 300-year-old recipe) are tiny but spicy, and the satin-smooth hot pumpkin soup drizzled with cheese may as well be dessert. *Wilhelminastraat 18A, Oranjestad, tel. 297/8–31888. AE, MC, V. No lunch Sun.*

$–$$ **The Paddock.** This typical Dutch *eet-café* (a café that serves full meals) is a casual open-air terrace overlooking the pier and whichever cruise ships happen to be in port (it's a favorite with the crews and sailors from around the world). French bread with Brie, fried eggs, bami goreng, saté, and fresh seafood salads are among the offerings. All-you-can-eat spareribs ($10) are the specials on Wednesday. *L. G. Smith Blvd. 13, Oranjestad, tel. 297/8–32334. MC, V.*

$ **Le Petit Café.** The motto here is "Romancing the Stone"—referring to tasty cuisine cooked on hot stones. The low ceiling and hanging plants make this an intimate lunch spot. Alfresco dining in the bustling square lets you keep an eye on things, but fumes from nearby traffic might spoil a streetside meal. Jumbo shrimp, sandwiches, ice cream, and fresh fruit are light delights. *Emmastraat 1, Oranjestad, tel. 297/8–26577. AE, DC, MC, V. No lunch Sun.*

Barbados

Barbados is a sophisticated island and life here doesn't skip a beat once cruise passengers have returned to their ships. A resort island since the 1700s, Barbados has cultivated a civilized attitude toward tourists.

Under uninterrupted British rule for 340 years—until independence in 1966—Barbados retains a very British atmosphere. Afternoon tea is a ritual, and cricket is the national sport. The atmosphere, though, is hardly stuffy.

Beaches along the island's south and west coasts are postcard-perfect, and all are open to cruise passengers. On the rugged east coast, where Bajans (as people in Barbados call themselves) have their own vacation homes, the Atlantic Ocean attracts world-class surfers. The northeast is dominated by rolling hills and valleys; the interior of the island is covered by acres of sugarcane and dotted with small villages. Historic plantations, a stalactite-studded cave, a wildlife preserve, rum factories, and tropical gardens are among the island's attractions, but Bridgetown, the capital, is a busy city with more traffic than charm.

Currency

One Barbados dollar (BDS$) equals about U.S.50¢. Either currency is accepted everywhere on the island, as are major credit cards and traveler's checks. Always ask which currency is being quoted. All prices given below are in U.S. dollars unless otherwise indicated.

Telephones

Local calls cost BDS25¢ per five minutes from a public pay phone. Prepaid phone cards are available at the cruise-ship terminal. To place a call to the United States, use the same direct-dialing procedure as you would at home. To charge an international call to a major credit card at direct-dialing rates, dial 800/744–2000.

Shore Excursions

The following are good choices on Barbados. They may not be offered by all cruise lines. Times and prices are approximate.

Harrison's Cave and Island Tour. After a bus tour of the island, passengers board an electric tram for a one-hour tour
of this series of limestone caves. A highlight is the 40-ft underground waterfall that plunges into a deep underground
pool. *4 hrs. Cost: $52.*

Atlantis **Submarine.** A 50-ft sub dives as deep as 150 ft below
the surface for an exciting view of Barbados's profuse marine life. Most passengers find this trip to the depths—without getting wet—to be thrilling. *1½ hrs. Cost: $82.*

Coming Ashore

Up to eight ships at a time can dock at Bridgetown's Deep
Water Harbour, on the northwest side of Carlisle Bay. The
cruise-ship terminal has duty-free shops, handicraft vendors,
a post office, a telephone station, a tourist information desk,
and a taxi stand. To get downtown, follow the shoreline
to the Careenage. On foot it will take you about 15 minutes; you could also take a cab for $3 each way.

Taxis await ships at the pier. The fare to Needham's Point,
just south of Bridgetown, runs about $5; to Paynes Bay or
Holetown, it's $10. Drivers accept U.S. dollars and appreciate
a 10% tip. Taxis operate at a fixed hourly rate of $17.50
per carload (up to three passengers fit comfortably) and drivers will cheerfully narrate an island tour.

Exploring Barbados

*Numbers in the margin correspond to points of interest on
the Barbados map.*

The narrow strip of sea known as the Careenage made early
❶ Bridgetown a natural harbor. In the old days, this is where
working schooners were careened (turned on their sides),
scraped of barnacles, and repainted. Today, the Careenage
serves mainly as a marina for pleasure craft.

At the center of the bustling city is **Trafalgar Square.** The
monument to Lord Nelson predates its London counter-
part by about two decades. Also here are a war memorial
and a three-dolphin fountain that commemorates the advent of running water in Barbados in 1865.

The **Parliament Buildings** (circa 1870) house the third-oldest parliament of the British Commonwealth and are adjacent to Trafalgar Square. Stained-glass windows depicting British monarchs adorn these Victorian buildings.

George Washington is said to have worshiped at **St. Michael's Cathedral** on his only trip outside the United States. The structure was nearly a century old when he visited in 1751; destroyed twice by hurricanes, it was rebuilt in 1784 and 1831.

Queen's Park, northeast of downtown Bridgetown, is the site of an immense baobab tree more than 10 centuries old. The historic Queen's Park House, former home of the commander of the British troops, has been converted into a theater and a restaurant (open daily 9–5).

The intriguing **Barbados Museum** (about 1½ km/1 mi south of downtown Bridgetown on Highway 7) has artifacts dating from Arawak days (around 400 BC), mementos of military history and everyday life in the 19th century, wildlife and natural history exhibits, a well-stocked gift shop, and a good café. *Garrison Savannah, tel. 246/427–0201. Admission: $5 Open Mon.–Sat. 9–5, Sun. 2–6.*

CENTRAL BARBADOS/WEST COAST

② **Tyrol Cot Heritage Village,** just south of Bridgetown, is a historic home constructed in 1854 and now the centerpiece of an outdoor "living" museum: colorful chattel houses all have a traditional artisan or craftsman at work inside. The crafts are for sale, and refreshments are available at the "rum shop." *St. Michael, tel. 246/424–2074 or 246/436–9033. Admission: $5. Open weekdays 9–5.*

③ **Folkestone Marine Park** has a museum of marine life, public tennis courts, and a snorkeling trail around Dottin's Reef. A sunken barge is home to myriad fish. *Hwy. 1, north of Holetown, St. James, tel. 246/422–2314. Admission: 60¢. Open weekdays 9–5.*

④ **Harrison's Cave,** a series of beautiful limestone caverns, complete with subterranean streams and a 40-ft waterfall, is toured via electric tram. *Hwy. 2, St. Thomas, tel. 246/438–6640. Admission: $7.50. Open daily 9–6.*

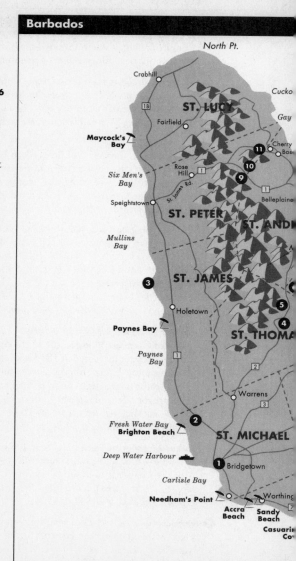

Barbados

North Pt.

Crabhill

ST. LUCY

Fairfield

Cucko

Gay

Maycock's Bay

Cherry
Bos

Six Men's
Bay

Rose
Hill

St. James Rd.

Speightstown

Belleplaine

ST. PETER

ST. AND

Mullins
Bay

ST. JAMES

ST. ANDI

Holetown

Paynes Bay

ST. THOMA

Paynes
Bay

Warrens

Fresh Water Bay
Brighton Beach

ST. MICHAEL

Deep Water Harbour

Bridgetown

Carlisle Bay

Needham's Point

Worthing

Accra
Beach

Sandy
Beach

Casuari
Co

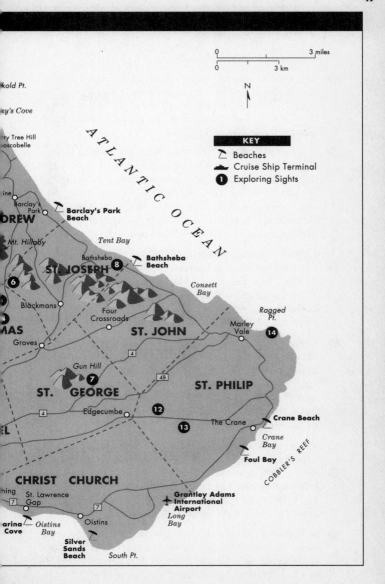

kold Pt.

ay's Cove

ry Tree Hill
oscobelle

ine

ATLANTIC OCEAN

Barclay's Park

Barclay's Park Beach

DREW

Mt. Hillaby

Tent Bay

ST. JOSEPH

Bathsheba 8

Bathsheba Beach

Consett Bay

6

Blackmans

Four Crossroads

ST. JOHN

Marley Vale

Ragged Pt.

14

MAS

Groves

4

Gun Hill

7

ST. GEORGE

48

ST. PHILIP

12

EL

4

Edgecumbe

13

The Crane

Crane Beach

Crane Bay

Foul Bay

COBBLER'S REEF

CHRIST CHURCH

hing

St. Lawrence Gap

7

arina Cove

Oistins Bay

Oistins

Silver Sands Beach

South Pt.

Grantley Adams International Airport

Long Bay

KEY

Beaches

Cruise Ship Terminal

1 Exploring Sights

0 — 3 miles

0 — 3 km

N

5 At **Welchman Hall Gully** you can explore acres of labeled flowers, see an occasional green monkey, and enjoy the peace and quiet. *Hwy. 2, St. Thomas, tel. 246/438–6671. Admission: $6. Open daily 9–5.*

6 At the **Flower Forest,** you can meander through 8 acres of fragrant bushes, canna and ginger lilies, puffball trees, and more than 100 other species of flora in a tranquil setting. *Hwy. 2, Richmond Plantation, St. Joseph, tel. 246/433–8152. Admission: $7. Open daily 9–5.*

7 The 360-degree view from **Gun Hill Signal Station** is what made this a site of such strategic importance to the 18th-century British army. Fields of green and gold extend all the way to the horizon, and brilliant flowers surround a picturesque gun tower. The white limestone lion just below the garrison is a famous landmark. *St. George, tel. 246/429–1358. Admission: $5. Open Mon.–Sat. 9–5.*

NORTHERN BARBADOS/EAST COAST

8 The small but fascinating **Andromeda Gardens,** set into cliffs that spill into the Atlantic Ocean on the east coast, are planted with unusual specimens from around the world. *Bathsheba, St. Joseph, tel. 246/433–9384. Admission: $6. Open daily 9–5.*

9 At **Farley Hill,** a national park, you can roam through the imposing ruins of a once-magnificent plantation house and its surrounding gardens, lawns, and towering royal palms. From the back of the estate, there's a sweeping view of the area of Barbados called Scotland because of its rugged landscape. *St. Peter, no phone. Admission: $1.50 per car, walkers free. Open daily 8:30–6.*

You'll encounter herons, land turtles, screeching peacocks, innumerable green monkeys, geese, brilliantly colored par-
10 rots, a kangaroo, and a friendly otter at the **Barbados Wildlife Reserve.** The fauna roam freely, so step carefully and keep your hands to yourself. *Farley Hill, St. Peter, tel. 246/422–8826. Admission: $10. Open daily 10–5.*

11 **St. Nicholas Abbey** is the oldest house on the island (circa 1650) and worth visiting for its Jacobean stone and wood architecture. *Near Cherry Tree Hill, St. Lucy, tel. 246/422–8725. Admission: $2.50. Open weekdays 10–3:30.*

⑫ **Sunbury Plantation House & Museum** has been lovingly re-built after a 1995 fire destroyed everything but its 2½-ft thick walls. This 300-year-old plantation house is once again an elegant representation of life on a Barbados sugar estate in the 18th and 19th centuries. A Bajan buffet lunch is served on the back patio. *St. Philip, tel. 246/423–6270. Admission: $5 tour only, $12.50 with lunch. Open daily 10–5.*

⑬ The **Rum Factory & Heritage Park** is a theme park that com-bines an operating high-tech rum distillery, the first to be built in Barbados in this century, with activities that show-case Bajan art, skills, and talents. Vendor carts and shops display local products, crafts, and foods. *Foursquare Sugar Plantation, St. Philip, tel. 246/420–1977. Admission: $12. Open daily 9–5.*

Shopping

Duty-free shopping is found in Bridgetown's Broad Street department stores and their branches at the cruise-ship ter-minal. (Note that to purchase items duty-free, you must show your passport). Stores are generally open weekdays 8:30–4:30 and Saturdays 8:30–1.

For antiques and fine memorabilia, try **Greenwich House An-tiques** (Greenwich Village, Trents Hill, St. James, tel. 246/432–1169). **Antiquaria** (Spring Garden Hwy., St. Michael's Row next to Anglican cathedral, Bridgetown, tel. 246/426–0635) is another good place to search for antiques. **Colours of De Caribbean** (On the wharf, Bridgetown, tel. 246/436–8522) is worth visiting for its original—and expensive—handmade clothing and accessories. At Bridgetown's **Pelican Village Handicrafts Center** (Princess Alice Hwy. near Cheap-side Market, tel. 246/426–4391) you can watch Bajan goods and crafts being made before you purchase them; woven straw rugs and mats are particularly good buys. **Earthworks** (Edge-hill Heights No. 2, St. Thomas, tel. 246/425–0223) is a fam-ily-owned pottery studio where you can watch the potters at work and purchase anything from a dish or knickknack to a complete dinner service. There are two **Chattel House Village** complexes (St. Lawrence Gap and Holetown), each a cluster of shops in brightly colored chattel houses. At **Best of Barbados** (tel. 246/436–1416), you'll find local products. Other shops sell clothing, beachwear, and souvenirs.

Sports

FISHING

Billfisher II (tel. 246/431–0741), a 40-ft Pacemaker, accommodates up to six people for half-day fishing trips. **Blue Jay Charters** (tel. 246/422–2098) has a fully equipped 45-ft fishing boat with a knowledgeable crew. Four fishermen can be accommodated, and each can invite a guest.

GOLF

On the southeast coast, **Club Rockley Barbados** (tel. 246/435– 7873) is a 9-hole course that can be played as 18, and the greens fee is $22.50. **Sandy Lane Golf Club** (tel. 246/432–1145) has undergone a dramatic redesign; the greens fee on this classic 18-hole course is $125.

HORSEBACK RIDING

The **Caribbean International Riding Center** (St. Joseph, tel. 246/433–1246) offers scenic trail rides, beginning at $40 for 1 hour, including transportation.

WATER SPORTS

Waterskiing, snorkeling, and parasailing are available on most beaches along the west and south coasts. Windsurfing is best at **Silver Sands Beach,** near the southern tip of the island where the winds are strongest. For scuba divers, Barbados is a rich and varied underwater destination. Reputable dive operators include the **Dive Shop Ltd.** (Aquatic Gap, near Grand Barbados Beach Resort, St. Michael, tel. 246/426–9947), **Dive Boat Safari** (Barbados Hilton, St. Michael, tel. 246/427–4350), and **Hightide Watersports** (Sandy Lane Hotel, St. James, tel. 246/432–0931).

Beaches

All beaches in Barbados are open to cruise-ship passengers. The west coast has the stunning coves and white-sand beaches dear to the hearts of postcard publishers, plus calm, clear water for snorkeling, scuba diving, and swimming. **Paynes Bay,** south of Holetown, is the site of several fine resorts; public access to the beach is easiest opposite the Coach House Pub. **Greave's End Beach,** south of Bridgetown at Aquatic Gap, is convenient and good for swimming. On the south coast, **Needham's Point Beach,** at the south end of Carlisle Bay, has changing rooms and showers. **Accra Beach,** in Rockley, is a popular beach, with water-sports equipment rental and snacks available. If you don't mind a drive across the island along Highway 7, **Crane Beach,** where the Atlantic meets the Caribbean, is a great find. Waves pound in and the sand is pink, but the water can be rough for swimming. The Crane Beach Hotel, on the cliff above the beach, charges $2.50 per person for access to the beach and changing facilities.

Dining

A 15% VAT (value-added tax) has been instituted in Barbados. Check restaurant menus to see whether the prices are VAT-inclusive or subject to the additional tax. A 10% service charge is added to most restaurant bills; if no service charge is added, tip waiters 10%–15%.

$–$$ **Waterfront Cafe.** A sidewalk table overlooking the Careenage is the perfect place to enjoy a drink, snack, burger, or Bajan meal. This popular bistro is a gathering place for locals and tourists alike. *Bridge House, Bridgetown, tel. 246/ 427–0093. MC, V. Closed Sun.*

$ **Atlantis Hotel.** When you tour the rugged east coast, plan to arrive at lunchtime for the enormous Bajan buffet, with pumpkin fritters, fried flying fish, roast chicken, pepper-pot stew, and more—along with a spectacular view of the Atlantic surf—all for about $12.50 per person (more on Sundays). *Bathsheba, St. Joseph, tel. 246/433–9445. AE.*

$ **Bomba's Beach Bar & Restaurant.** On the beach at Paynes Bay, Bomba's serves Bajan specialties, veggie food (fabulous avocado salad), and drinks made with fresh fruit juice—all whipped up by a Scottish chef and his Rasta partner. All dishes are less than $10. *Paynes Bay, St. James, tel. 246/432–0569. MC, V.*

$ **Sunbury Plantation House.** In the patio behind the restored great house, luncheon is served to visitors as part of the house tour. The Bajan buffet includes baked chicken and fish, salads, rice and peas, steamed local vegetables, and dessert. Sandwiches are available, too. *Off Hwy., near Six Cross Rd., St. Philip, tel. 246/423–6270. AE, MC, V.*

Cozumel, Mexico

Cozumel, with its sun-drenched ivory beaches fringed with coral reefs, fulfills the tourist's vision of a tropical Caribbean island. More relaxed and less developed than Cancún, Cozumel surpasses its fancier neighbor in many ways. It has more history, lovelier and more secluded beaches, superior diving and snorkeling, more authentic cuisine, and a greater diversity of handicrafts at better prices.

The island is a heady mix of the natural and the commercial. Most of the island is undeveloped; San Miguel is its one city. The numerous coral reefs, particularly the world-renowned Palancar Reef, attract divers from around the world. Cozumel is also the mainstay for ships sailing on western Caribbean itineraries, and as a result the island has grown more commercial. Waterfront shops and restaurants have taken on a more glitzy appearance—gone are the hole-in-the-wall crafts shops and little diners, replaced by high-dollar duty-free shops, gem traders, and slick eateries. There are also no fewer than half a dozen American fast-food chains as well as a Hard Rock Café and Planet Hollywood. The duty-free shops stay open as long as a ship is in town, and most of the salespeople speak English.

Cruise ships visiting for just one day normally call only at Cozumel; ships staying for two days usually call at Cozumel on one day and on the other anchor off Playa del Carmen, across the channel on the Yucatán Peninsula. From there, excursions go to Cancún or to the Mayan ruins at Tulum, Cobá, and Chichén Itzá.

Currency

In Mexico the currency is the peso, designated as MX$. At press time, the exchange rate was about MX$9.50 to US$1. Most prices given below are in U.S. dollars.

U.S. dollars and credit cards are accepted at most restaurants and large shops. Most taxi drivers take dollars as well. There is no advantage to paying in dollars, but there may be an advantage to paying in cash. To avoid having to change unused pesos back to dollars, change just enough to cover what you'll need for public transportation, refreshments, phones, and tips.

Telephones

The best place to make long-distance calls is at the Calling Station (Av. Melgar 27 and Calle 3 S, tel. 987/2–14–17), where you'll save 10%–50%. You can also exchange money here. It is open mid-December–April, daily 8 AM–11 PM; the rest of the year, it's open Monday–Saturday 9 AM–10 PM and Sunday 9–1 and 5–10.

Shore Excursions

The following are good choices in Cozumel. They may not be offered by all cruise lines. Times and prices are approximate.

ARCHAEOLOGICAL SITES

Chichén Itzá. This incredible and awe-inspiring ruin of a great Maya city is a 45-minute flight from Cozumel or a 12-hour round-trip bus ride from Playa del Carmen. A box lunch is included. *Full day. Cost: $200 (by plane), $85 (by bus).*

San Gervasio and Cozumel Island. If you want to see Maya ruins but don't want to spend a full day on a tour, this excursion to a local archaeological site is a good alternative. Time is also allotted for swimming and snorkeling at the Playa Sol beach. *4 hrs. Cost: $36.*

Tulum Ruins and Xel-ha Lagoon. An English-speaking guide leads a tour to this superbly preserved ancient Maya city, perched on the cliffs above a beautiful beach. A box lunch is usually included. A stop is made for a swim and snorkeling in the glass-clear waters of Xel-ha. The tour leaves from Playa del Carmen. *6 hrs. Cost: $80.*

UNDERSEA CREATURES

Glass-Bottom Boat. For those who don't dive, a tour boat with a see-through floor takes passengers to the famed Paraiso and Chankanaab sites to view schools of tropical fish. *2 hrs. Cost: $37.*

Snorkeling. This region is famous for its reefs. Originally discovered by Jacques Cousteau, it is regularly featured in *Skin Diver* magazine as one of the top diving destinations in the world. If your ship offers a snorkeling tour, take it. Equipment and lessons are included. *3 hrs. Cost: $29.*

Coming Ashore

As many as six ships call at Cozumel on a busy day, tendering passengers to the downtown pier in the center of San Miguel or docking at the international pier 6 km (4 mi) away. From the downtown pier you can walk into town or catch the ferry to Playa del Carmen. Taxi tours are also available.

Sample prices are $7 to the Chankanaab Nature Park, $12 to the Playa Sol beach, and $35 to the Maya ruins at San Gervasio. An island tour, including the ruins and other sights, costs about $60. The international pier is close to many beaches, but you'll need a taxi to get into town. Fortunately, cabs meet incoming ships, so there's rarely a wait. Expect to pay $4 for the ride into San Miguel from the pier.

Once in town, you can find a tourist information directory on the main square, immediately across from the downtown pier, and at the State Tourism Office in the Plaza del Sol mall at the east end of the square (tel. 987/2–09–72); it's open weekdays 9–2:30. To get to Playa del Carmen from Cozumel, you can take a ferry or a jetfoil from the downtown pier. It costs about $10 round-trip and takes 30–40 minutes each way. Ferries depart every hour or two; the last ferry back to Cozumel leaves around 8:30 PM, but be sure to double-check because the schedule changes frequently.

Exploring Cozumel

San Miguel is tiny—you cannot get lost—and best explored on foot. The main attractions are the small eateries and shops that line the streets. Activity centers on the ferry and the main square, where the locals congregate in the evenings. The lovely **Museo de la Isla de Cozumel,** located along the main road near the ferry docks, has exhibits explaining the island's environment and ecosystems on the first floor. Upstairs are historical exhibits and artifacts from the island's colonial era as well as a display on Maya life. The museum has a pleasant café as well. *Av. Melgar and Calle 4 N, tel. 987/2–14–75. Admission: $3. Open daily 10–6.*

To see the largest Maya and Toltec site on Cozumel, head inland to the jungle. The ruins at **San Gervasio** once served as the island's capital and its ceremonial center, dedicated to the fertility goddess Ixchel. What remains today are numerous ruins scattered around a plaza and a main road leading to the sea (probably a major trade route). Because the ruins are clearly marked, a guide is not necessary but will certainly enhance your tour. Guides charge $12 for groups of up to six, so try to organize a group aboard ship. If you prefer to go solo, visit the museum for information on the ruins that's as good as you'll get from a guide. *Admission: $1 to private road, $3.50 for ruins. Open daily 8–5.*

To sample Cozumel's natural beauty, head south out of town on Avenida Rafael Melgar; after 11 km (6½ mi) your first stop will be the **Chankanaab Nature Park.** This natural aquarium has been designated an underwater preserve for more than 50 species of tropical fish, as well as crustaceans and coral. Snorkeling and scuba equipment can be rented, and instruction and professional guides are available. Park facilities include gift shops, snack bars, and a restaurant serving fresh seafood. You'll also find reproductions of Maya ruins and a botanical garden with 350 species of plant life from 20 countries. *No phone. Admission: $7. Open daily 6–5:30; restaurant open daily 10–5.*

Shopping

San Miguel's biggest industry—even bigger than diving— is selling souvenirs to cruise-ship passengers. The primary items are ceramics, onyx, brass, wood carvings, colorful blankets and hammocks, reproductions of Maya artifacts, shells, silver, gold, sportswear, T-shirts, perfume, and liquor. Look for Mexican pewter; it's unusual, affordable, and attractive. Almost all stores take U.S. dollars.

Before you spend any serious cash, though, keep in mind the following tips. Don't pay attention to written or verbal offers of "20% discount, today only" or "only for cruise ship passengers"—they're nothing but bait to get you inside. Similarly, many of the larger stores advertise "duty-free" wares, but prices tend to be higher than retail prices in the United States. Avoid buying from street vendors as the quality of their merchandise can be questionable, which may not be apparent until it's too late. Don't buy anything from the black coral "factories." The items are overpriced and black coral is an endangered species.

The center of the shopping district is the main square off Avenida Melgar, across from the ferry terminal. The district extends north along Avenida Melgar and Calles 5 Sur and Norte. As a general rule, the newer, trendier shops line the waterfront, and the better crafts shops can be found around Avenida 5a. A **crafts market** on Calle 1 Sur, behind the plaza, sells a respectable assortment of Mexican wares. **Los Cincos Soles** (Av. Melgar N 27) has a number of shops catering to cruise ships. Other plazas include **Plaza del Sol** (on the east side of the main plaza), **Villa Mar** (on the north side of the main plaza), the **Plaza Confetti** (on the south side of the main plaza). The most bizarre collection of shops selling Maya figures, masks, rare coins, and liquor can be found at the **Cozumel Flea Market** on Avenida 5 between Calles 2 and 4. For local atmosphere, fresh fruit, and other foods try the **Municipal Market** (Av. 25 S and Calle Salas). **La Fiesta Cozumel** (Av. Melgar N 164-B), a large store that caters to cruise passengers, sells T-shirts and souvenirs. Cozumel is famous for its jewelry—gold, silver, and with precious and semiprecious gemstones—and some great bargains can be had if you're prepared to shop around. **Diamond Creations, Joyeria Palancar,** and **Van Cleef & Arpels** have shops along the waterfront. Look for good deals at **Cozumel Silver & Gold Exchange** (Av. 5 S 201-A). There are also a number of shops at the cruise-ship terminal near the Casa Del Mar, La Ceiba, and Sol Caribe hotels.

If your ship docks at the International Pier, you can shop dockside for T-shirts, crafts, and more.

Sports

FISHING

In Cozumel contact **Yucab Reef Diving and Fishing Center** (tel. 987/2–41–10) or **Club Naútico Cozumel** (tel. 987/2–01–18; 800/253–2701 in the U.S.).

SCUBA DIVING AND SNORKELING

Cozumel is famous for its reefs. In addition to **Chankanaab Nature Park** (*see* Exploring Cozumel, *above*), another great dive site is **La Ceiba Reef,** in the waters off La Ceiba and Sol Caribe hotels. Here lies the wreckage of a sunken airplane that was blown up for a Mexican disaster movie. Cozumel's dive shops include **Aqua Safari** (tel. 987/2–01–01), **Blue Angel** (tel. 987/2–16–31), **Dive Paradise** (tel. 987/2–10–07), **Eagle Ray Dive School** (tel. 987/2–57–35), **Fantasia Divers** (tel. 987/2–28–40; 800/336–3483 in the U.S.), and **Michelle's Dive Shop** (tel. 987/2–09–47).

Dining

Although it is not common in Mexico, a 10%–15% service charge may be added to the bill. Otherwise, a 10%–20% tip is customary.

$$ **La Choza.** With its white stucco walls, open kitchen, and thatched roof, this family-run restaurant resembles a large

Maya home. The informal patio is furnished with simple wood tables and chairs, oilcloth table coverings, and hand-painted pottery dishes. Dona Elisa Espinosa is accompanied in the kitchen by her daughter; together they create culinary magic. Be sure to try the chilies stuffed with shrimp or the *pollo en relleno negro* (chicken in a blackened chili sauce) and the cool, refreshing avocado pie. *Calle Salas 198 at Av. 10a S, tel. 987/2–09–58. AE, MC, V.*

$$ **Prima.** On a breezy second-floor terrace is the best Italian restaurant on the island. Everything is fresh and the vegetables are grown by the owner. The menu changes daily and may include angel-hair pasta with lobster and sun-dried tomatoes or crab ravioli with cream sauce. The puff-pastry garlic bread is sublime. Downstairs is a store where you'll find Mexico's finest wines alongside Cuban cigars. Next door, Prima Deli packs a great lunch. *Calle Salas 109, tel. 987/2–42–42 or 987/2–24–77. MC, V.*

$ **El Foco.** Ready to try some traditional Mexican food? Head to this little *taquería* (taco stand). Start with the soft tacos stuffed with pork, or chorizo, cheese, or chilies. You can also get a good rack of ribs. The graffiti on the walls makes for a fun diversion while you eat. *Av. 5 S 13-B, between Calle Salas and Calle 3, no phone. No credit cards.*

$ **Jeanie's Waffle House.** This place is usually packed but the wait is worth it. Jeanie De Lille, the island's premier pastry chef, creates amazingly light waffles served any way you want them. Make sure to try the fruit- and nut-filled waffles. Also on the menu are eggs, hash browns, homemade breads, and great coffee. Breakfast is served all day along with a lunch and dinner menu that includes fried fish, tamales, and several pasta dishes. *In the Vista del Mar Hotel, Av. Melgar, tel. 987/2–05–45. AE, MC, V.*

Nightlife

Cozumel is not exactly known for its nightlife, but there are a few places to party. For a quiet drink and some people-watching, try **Video Bar Aladino** at the San Miguel Hotel at the northern end of the plaza. Pass an evening with a pint of beer and a game of darts at **Scruffy Murphy's Irish Pub** (Calle Salas, tel. 987/2–11–54). Serious bar-hoppers like **Carlos 'n' Charlie's** (Av. Melgar 11, between Calles 2 and 4 N, tel. 987/2–01–91) and **Sharkey's** (Av. Melgar near Av. Benito Juárez, tel. 987/2–18–32). The **Hard Rock Café**

(Av. Melgar 2A, near Av. Benito Juárez, tel. 987/2–52–71) and **Planet Hollywood** (Av. Melgar 161, tel. 987/2–57–95) serve the usual American grub you've come to expect from these international chains. You and your friends provide the entertainment at the sing-along **Laser-Karaoke Bar** (Fiesta Inn, tel. 987/2–28–11). Sports fans will enjoy the **Sports Page Video Bar and Restaurant** (Av. 5 N and Calle 2 N, tel. 987/2–11–99). **Hooks Restaurant, Bar & Disco** (Calle Salas at Av. 5 and Av. Melgar) has a disco open from Thursday to Saturday, as does **Neptuno** (Av. Melgar at Calle 11 S, tel. 987/2–15–37), although things are pretty quiet there on weekdays.

Curaçao

Try to be on deck as your ship sails into Curaçao. The tiny Queen Emma Floating Bridge swings aside to open the narrow channel. Pastel gingerbread buildings on shore look like dollhouses, especially from a large cruise ship. Although the gabled roofs and red tiles show a Dutch influence, the riotous colors of the facades are peculiar to Curaçao. It's said that an early governor of the island suffered from migraines that were aggravated by the color white, so all the houses were painted in hues from magenta to mauve.

Fifty-six kilometers (35 miles) north of Venezuela and 67 km (42 mi) east of Aruba, Curaçao is, at 61 km (38 mi) long and 5–12 km (3–7½ mi) wide, the largest of the Netherlands Antilles. Although always sunny, it's never stiflingly hot here because of the constant trade winds. Water sports attract enthusiasts from all over the world, and the reef diving is excellent.

History books still don't agree as to whether Alonzo de Ojeda or Amerigo Vespucci discovered Curaçao, only that it happened around 1499. In 1634 the Dutch came and promptly shipped off the Spanish settlers and the few remaining Indians to Venezuela. To defend itself against French and British invasions, the city built massive ramparts, many of which now house unusual restaurants and hotels.

Today, Curaçao's population, which comprises more than 50 nationalities, is one of the best-educated in the Caribbean. The island is known for its religious tolerance, and tourists are warmly welcomed and almost never pestered by vendors and shopkeepers. Although there's plenty to see and do in Willemstad, the rest of the island features rugged natural beauty in the form of cramped champagne coves shadowed by gunmetal cliffs and a remarkable, beautifully preserved collection of *landhuisen,* or plantation land houses, all colored and many open to the public.

Currency

U.S. dollars are fine, so don't worry about exchanging money, except for pay phones. The local currency is the guilder or florin, indicated by "fl" or "NAf" on price tags. At press time, the exchange rate was NAf1.80 to US$1.

Telephones

The telephone system is reliable. To place a local call, dial the seven-digit number. Pay phones charge NAf.50 for a local call. If you need to place an international call, there's an overseas phone center in the cruise-ship terminal. Dialing to the United States is exactly the same as dialing long distance within the United States.

Shore Excursions

The following are good choices in Curaçao. They may not be offered by all cruise lines. Times and prices are approximate.

ISLAND SIGHTS

Country Drive. This is a good tour if you'd like to see Westpunt and Mt. Christoffel but don't want to risk driving an hour there yourself. Other stops are made at a land house, Hato Caves, and the Curaçao Museum. *3 hrs. Cost: $32.*

Willemstad Trolley Train. Although there are several walking tours of the charming capital, Willemstad, they're lengthy and detailed. The trolley visits such highlights as the Floating Market, the Synagogue, Ft. Amsterdam, and Waterloo Arches. *75 minutes. Cost: $21.*

UNDERSEA CREATURES

Sharks, Stingrays, and Shipwrecks. Curaçao's seaquarium, a marine park, and two sunken ships reached by a 30-minute submarine trip highlight this tour of the island's marine environment. *3 hrs. Cost: $39.*

Coming Ashore

Ships dock at the terminal just beyond the Queen Emma Bridge, which leads to the floating market and the shopping district. The walk to downtown takes less than 10 minutes. Easy-to-read maps are posted dockside and in the shopping area. The terminal has a duty-free shop, telephones, and a taxi stand. Taxis, which meet every ship, aren't metered, so confirm the fare before setting out. A taxi for up to four people will cost about $30 an hour.

Exploring Curaçao

Numbers in the margin correspond to points of interest on the Curaçao map.

WILLEMSTAD

❶ **Willemstad** is small and navigable on foot. You needn't spend more than two or three hours wandering around here, although the narrow alleys and various architectural styles are enchanting. English, Spanish, and Dutch are widely spoken. Narrow Santa Anna Bay divides the city into the Punda, where the main shopping district is, and the Otrabanda (literally, the "other side"), where the cruise ships dock. The Punda is crammed with shops, restaurants, monuments, and markets. The Otrabanda has narrow winding streets full of colonial homes notable for their gables and Dutch-influenced designs.

You can cross from the Otrabanda to the Punda in one of three ways: Walk over the Queen Emma Pontoon Bridge; ride the free ferry, which runs when the bridge swings open (at least 30 times a day) to let seagoing vessels pass; or take a cab across the Juliana Bridge (about $7). The first landmark that you'll come upon is the **Queen Emma Bridge,** which locals call the Lady. The toll for the original bridge, built in 1888, was 2¢ per person if wearing shoes and free if barefoot. Today it's free, no matter what's on your feet.

On the Punda side of the city, **Handelskade** is where you'll find Willemstad's most famous sights—the colorful colonial buildings that line the waterfront. The original red roof tiles came from Europe on trade ships as ballast.

The bustling, colorful, noisy **floating market** is on Sha Caprileskade. Each morning, dozens of Venezuelan schooners arrive laden with tropical fruits and vegetables. (Note that you should thoroughly wash and peel any produce you buy here before eating it.)

The Wilhelmina Drawbridge connects the Punda with once-flourishing **Scharloo**. The early Jewish merchants built stately homes in this district, and many of these intriguing structures (some from the 17th century) have been meticulously renovated by the government. If you cross the bridge to admire the architecture along Scharlooweg, steer clear of the waterfront end (Kleine Werf), which is a red-light district.

The Punda's **Mikveh Israel-Emmanuel Synagogue** was founded in 1651 and is the oldest temple still in use in the Western Hemisphere. It draws 20,000 visitors a year. Enter through the gates around the corner on Hanchi Di Snoa. A museum in the back displays Jewish antiques and fine Judaica. *Hanchi Di Snoa 29, tel. 5999/461–1067. Admission: $2. Open weekdays 9–11:45 and 2:30–4:45.*

At the end of Columbusstraat lies **Wilhelmina Park.** The statue keeping watch is of Queen Wilhelmina, the popular Dutch monarch who gave up her throne to her daughter Juliana in 1948. At the far side of the square is the impressive Georgian facade of the McLaughlin Bank and, to its right, the courthouse with its stately balustrade.

Guarding the waterfront at the foot of the Pontoon Bridge are the mustard-color walls of **Ft. Amsterdam;** take a few steps through the archway and enter another century. In the 1700s the structure was the center of the city and the most important fort on the island. Now it houses the governor's residence, the Fort Church, and other government offices. Outside the entrance, gnarled wayaka trees have fanciful carvings of a dragon, a squid, and a mermaid.

WESTERN CURAÇAO

The road that leads to the northwest tip of the island winds through landscape that Georgia O'Keeffe might have painted—towering cacti, flamboyant dried shrubbery, aluminum-roof houses. You may see fishermen hauling in their nets, women pounding cornmeal, and donkeys blocking traffic. You can often glimpse land houses from the road.

62

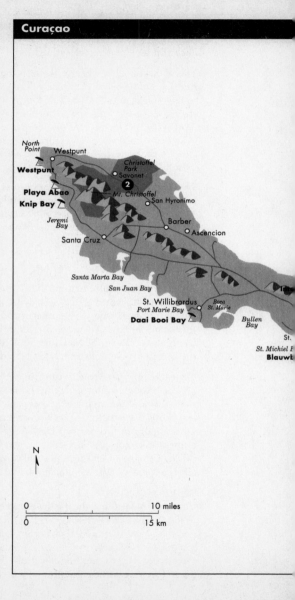

Curaçao

North
Point   Westpunt

Westpunt

Christoffel
Park
Savonet

2

Playa Abao
Knip Bay

Mt. Christoffel

San Hyronimo

Jeremi
Bay

Barber

Santa Cruz

Ascencion

Santa Marta Bay
San Juan Bay

St. Willibrordus
Port Marie Bay

Boca
St. Marie

Daai Booi Bay

Bullen
Bay

St.
St. Michiel P
Blauwk

N

0 ———————————— 10 miles
0 ———————————— 15 km

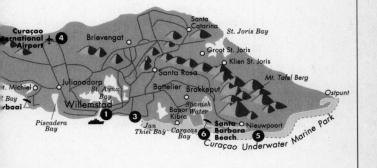

Caribbean Sea

Curaçao
International
Airport

Brievengat

Santa
Catarina

St. Joris Bay

Groot St. Joris

Klien St. Joris

Mt. Tafel Berg

Santa Rosa

Bottelier

Brakkeput

Ospunt

t. Michiel

Julianadorp

St. Anna
Bay

Willemstad

Bapor
Water

Spanish

Kibra

Nieuwpoort

Bay

ybaai

Piscadera
Bay

Jan
Thiel Bay

Caracas
Bay

Santa
Barbara
Beach

Curaçao Underwater Marine Park

KEY

Beaches

Cruise Ship Terminal

Exploring Sights

❷ **Christoffel Park** is a good hour from Willemstad (so watch the time) but worth a visit. This fantastic 4,450-acre garden and wildlife preserve with Mt. Christoffel at its center consists of three former plantations. As you drive through the park, watch for deer, goats, and other small wildlife that might suddenly dart in front of your car. If you skip everything else on the island, it's possible to drive to the park and climb 1,239-ft Mt. Christoffel, which takes two to three strenuous hours. The view from the peak is amazing—on a clear day you can even see the mountain ranges of Venezuela, Bonaire, and Aruba. *Savonet, tel. 5999/864–0363. Admission: $13.50. Open Mon.–Sat. 8–4, Sun. 6–3.*

EASTERN CURAÇAO

❸ At the **Curaçao Seaquarium,** more than 400 varieties of exotic fish and vegetation are displayed. Outside is a 1,623-ft-long artificial beach of white sand, well-suited to novice swimmers and children. There's also a platform that overlooks the wreck of the steamship SS *Oranje Nassau* and an underwater observatory where you can watch divers and snorkelers swimming with stingrays and feeding sharks. *Tel. 5999/461–6666. Admission: $13.25. Open daily 8:30–5:30.*

❹ Near the airport are the **Hato Caves,** where you can take an hour-long guided tour into water-pool chambers, a voodoo chamber, fruit bats' sleeping quarters, and Curaçao Falls—where a stream of silver joins a stream of gold. Hidden lights illuminate the limestone formations and gravel walkways. This is one of the better Caribbean caves open to the public. (Passengers with mobility problems should note that steep steps lead to the entrance.) *Tel. 5999/868–0379. Admission: $6.25. Open daily 10–5.*

❺ **Curaçao Underwater Marine Park** is the best spot for snorkeling—though the seabed is litter-strewn in places (*see* Sports, *below*). The park stretches along the southern shore, from Willemstad to the eastern tip of the island.

Along the southern shore, several private yacht clubs attract sports anglers from all over the world for international tournaments. Stop at Santa Barbara Beach, especially on
❻ Sunday, when the atmosphere approaches party time. **Caracas Bay** is a popular dive site, with a sunken ship so close to the surface that even snorkelers can view it clearly.

Shopping

Curaçao has some of the best shops in the Caribbean, but in many cases the prices are no lower than in U.S. discount stores. Hours are usually Monday–Saturday 8–noon and 2–6. Most shops are within the six-block area of Willemstad described above. The main shopping streets are Heerenstraat, Breedestraat, and Madurostraat, where you'll find **Bamali** (Waterfort Arches, tel. 5999/461–2258) for Indonesian batik clothing and leather. **Fundason Obra di Man** (Bargestraat 57, tel. 5999/461–2413) sells native crafts and curios, including marvelous posters and metal or ceramic renderings of typical landhuisen. If you've always longed for Dutch clogs, tulips, delftware, Dutch fashions, or chocolate, as well as, incongruously enough, craftwork from Latin America, try **Clog Dance** (De Rouvilleweg 9B, tel. 5999/462–3280).

Arawak Craft Factory (Mattheywerf 1, tel. 5999/462–7249), between the Queen Emma Bridge and the cruise-ship terminal, is open whenever ships are in port. You can buy tiles, plates, pots, and tiny land-house replicas here.

Julius L. Penha & Sons (Heerenstraat 1, tel. 5999/461–2266), in front of the Pontoon Bridge, sells French perfumes; Hummel figurines; linen from Madeira; delftware; and handbags from Argentina, Italy, and Spain. The store also has an extensive cosmetics counter. **Boolchand's** (Heerenstraat 4B, tel. 5999/461– 2262) handles an interesting variety of merchandise behind a facade of red-and-white-check tiles. Stock up here on French perfumes, British cashmere sweaters, Italian silk ties, Dutch dolls, Swiss watches, and Japanese cameras. **Little Switzerland** (Breedestraat 44, tel. 5999/461–2111) is the place for duty-free shopping. Here you'll find perfumes, jewelry, watches, crystal, china, and leather goods at significant savings. Try **New Amsterdam** (Gomezplein 14, tel. 5999/461–2469) for hand-embroidered tablecloths, napkins, and pillowcases. **La Casa Amarilla** (Breedestraat 46, tel 5999/461–3222) purveys premier perfumes and cosmetics from Poison to Passion.

Sports

HIKING

Christoffel Park has a number of challenging trails (*see* Exploring Curaçao, *above*).

SCUBA DIVING AND SNORKELING

The **Curaçao Underwater Marine Park** (tel. 5999/461–8131) is about 21 km (12½ mi) of untouched coral reef that has national park status. Mooring buoys mark the most interesting dive sites. If your cruise ship doesn't offer an excursion, contact **Curaçao Seascape** (tel. 5999/462–5000, ext. 6056), **Peter Hughes Divers** (tel. 5999/736–7888), or **Underwater Curaçao** (tel. 5999/461–8131).

Beaches

Curaçao doesn't have long, powdery stretches of sand. Instead you'll discover the joy of inlets: tiny bays marked by craggy cliffs, exotic trees, and scads of interesting pebbles and washed up coral. **Westpunt,** on the northwest tip of the island, is rocky, with very little sand, but shady in the morning and with a bay view worth the one-hour trip. On Sunday watch divers jump from the high cliff. **Knip Bay** has two parts: Groot (Big) Knip and Kleine (Little) Knip. Both have alluring white sand, but Kleine Knip is shaded by (highly poisonous) manchineel trees. Take the road to the Knip Landhouse, then turn right; signs will direct you.

Dining

Restaurants usually add a 10%–15% service charge.

$$ Bistro Le Clochard. This romantic gem is built into the 18th-century Riffort and is suffused with the cool, dark atmosphere of ages past. The use of fresh ingredients in consistently well-prepared French and Swiss dishes makes dining a dream. Try the fresh fish platters or the tender veal in mushroom sauce. Save room for the chocolate mousse. *Harbourside Terrace, Riffort Otrabunda, tel. 5999/462–5666. AE, DC, MC, V. Closed Sun. No lunch Sat.*

$–$$ Mambo Beach. This beach bar at the Seaquarium's artificial strand offers a lively, nonstop, party atmosphere and surprisingly creative seafood. You may try the dish named after Marilyn Monroe (smoked marlin in sun-dried tomato sauce) or the salmon fried in couscous with tomato and saffron; you could also opt for pastas and burgers. *Seaquarium Beach, tel. 5999/461–8999. AE, MC, V.*

Dominica

They say that if Christopher Columbus were to revisit the Caribbean islands today, Dominica is the only one he would recognize. In the center of the Caribbean arc, wedged between Guadeloupe to the north and Martinique to the south, Dominica (pronounced dom-in-*ee*-ka) is the most unspoiled island in today's Caribbean. In the luxuriant rain forest of her interior, wild orchids, anthurium lilies, ferns, heliconias, and myriad fruit trees sprout profusely; her rugged northwest is home to the last survivors of the region's original inhabitants, the Carib Indians. It's a wild place, straight out of Conan Doyle's *Lost World*. From the Elfin Woodlands which cover the mountains to the dense, luxuriant rain forest, Dominica is a slice of paradise.

Tiny Dominica—just 29 mi long and 16 mi wide—is an independent commonwealth with a seat in the United Nations. Its capital is Roseau (pronounced rose-*oh*), its official language is English, its roads are driven on the left. Most family and place names are French, and the most common religion is Catholicism. Unusual for the Caribbean, Dominica's economy is still based on agriculture and not yet on the tourist dollar. There may not be casinos or swim-up bars here, but if you want to take leave of everyday life— to hike into virgin forest, scuba dive, explore waterfalls and volcanic lakes—this is the place to do it.

Currency

The official currency is the Eastern Caribbean dollar (EC$). Figure about EC$2.70 to the US$1. U.S. dollars are readily accepted, but you will usually get change in E.C. dollars. Most major credit cards are accepted, as are traveler's checks. Prices throughout this chapter are quoted in U.S. dollars unless otherwise indicated.

Telephones

To place a local call on Dominica, you need to dial the seven-digit number that follows the area code. The island has efficient direct-dial international service. All pay phones are equipped for local and overseas dialing, and accept either E.C. coins or phone cards, which you can buy at many of the island's bars, restaurants, and shops.

Shore Excursions

The following are good choices in Dominica. They may not be offered by all cruise lines. Times and prices are approximate.

ISLAND SIGHTS

Carib Indian Cultural Tour. A bus will take you from Roseau to the Carib Indian Territory in northwest Dominica's Trois Pitons National Park. You'll learn about the history of the tribe and view a performance by the Karifouna Cultural Group. *5 hrs. Cost: $51.*

NATURAL BEAUTY

Mountain Biking Tour. Experience Dominica's interior via mountain bike as you ride along the southwest coast, past Morne Trois Pitons, to a secluded hot-water pool. *3 ½ hrs. Cost: $70.*

Roseau and Emerald Pool Tour. From Roseau, you'll travel through the Botanic Gardens to the Emerald Pool, in the heart of the rain forest. Take a swim in the chilly waterfall, then experience a folkloric performance at a hotel before returning to Roseau. *4 hrs. Cost: $30.*

UNDERSEA CREATURES

Dominica Snorkel and Scuba Tours. Snorkel or dive at Champagne Reef, where an underwater geothermal vent gives off bubbles. Diving tours may be restricted to passengers with certification. *3 hrs. Cost: $29 (snorkeling), $51 (diving).*

Coming Ashore

In Roseau, most ships dock along the Bayfront. Across the street from the pier, in the old post-office building, is a visitor information office.

Taxis, minibuses, and organized tours are available right here. The taxi drivers and tour guides can be overanxious to take you on a minibus or walking tour of Roseau. If you do decide to tour with one of them (it is safe), be courteous, explicit, and firm when discussing where you will go and how much you will pay—don't be afraid to ask questions. The drivers usually quote a fixed fare, but there is almost always room for negotiation. Expect to pay about $20 per hour for an island tour.

Some ships berth at the dock in Cabrits National Park, just north of Portsmouth. Portsmouth is quieter than Roseau, and in close proximity to some of Dominica's best nature sites, hikes, and river and beach bathing. The cruise-ship facility offers a co-operative crafts shop, a continuously screened film about Ft. Shirley, and the occasional live dance or music performance. As in Roseau, taxi and minibus drivers meet arriving ships right near the dock. Prices are comparable to those in Roseau.

Exploring Dominica

Although almond-shape Dominica is small, most of her roads are quite narrow and winding, and you'll need a few hours to take in the sights. Be adventurous, whether you prefer sightseeing or hiking—you'll be amply rewarded.

Numbers in the margin correspond to points of interest on the Dominica map.

① **Roseau** is one of the smallest capital cities in the Caribbean. Its wood-and-stone houses, with their brightly painted shutters, and its bustling marketplace transport you to an earlier time. Although you could walk the entire town in about an hour, on a more leisurely stroll you'll get a much better feel for the place. Don't be intimidated by the locals' eagerness to make friends; Dominicans are reputed to be some of the warmest people in this part of the world.

Across from the cruise-ship pier, in the old post-office building (next to the tourism office), is the **Dominica Museum.** In the heart of Roseau's French Quarter, the museum contains furnishings, documents, prints, and maps that date back hundreds of years. *Dame M. E. Charles Blvd. Admission: $2. Open Mon.–Fri. 9–4, Sat. 9–noon.*

A five-minute walk from Roseau's docks are the 40-acre **②** **Botanical Gardens,** founded in 1891 as an annex of London's Kew Gardens. In addition to the extensive collection of tropical plants and trees, there's a parrot aviary. At the forestry division's office, also on the grounds, you'll find information about the island's flora, fauna, and national parks. If you're going to spend any time walking around Roseau, this is a must-see. You can expect your visit to take about 45 minutes. *Tel. 767/448–2401, ext. 3417. Open Mon. 8–1 and 2–5, Tues.–Fri. 8–1 and 2–4.*

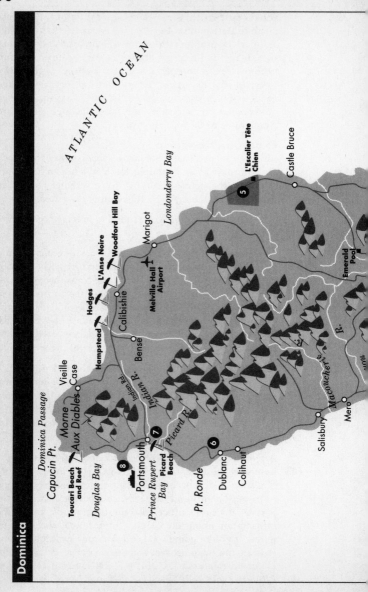

Dominica

ATLANTIC OCEAN

Capucin Pt.
Dominica Passage
Vieille
Morne
Aux Diables Case
Toucari Beach
and Reef
Douglas Bay
Portsmouth
Prince Rupert Bay
Picard Beach
Picard R.
Pt. Ronde
Dublanc
Colihaut
Indian R.
Bense
Hampstead
Hodges
Colibishie
L'Anse Noire
Woodford Hill Bay
Marigot
Londonderry Bay
Melville Hall Airport
L'Escalier Tête Chien
Castle Bruce
Emerald Pool
Salisbury
Mero
Macouchie R.

5
6
7
8

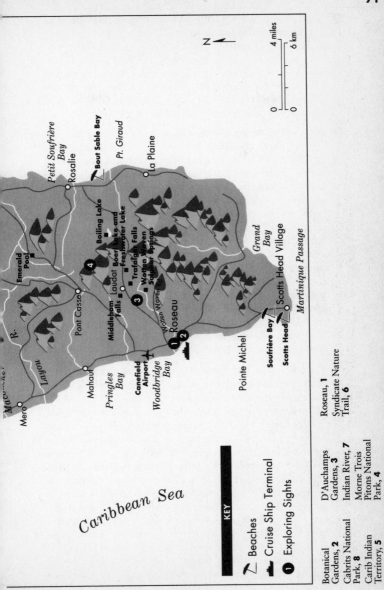

KEY

⊿ Beaches

⚓ Cruise Ship Terminal

❶ Exploring Sights

Botanical Gardens, **2**
Cabrits National Park, **8**
Carib Indian Territory, **5**
D'Auchamps Gardens, **3**
Indian River, **7**
Morne Trois Pitons National Park, **4**
Roseau, **1**
Syndicate Nature Trail, **6**

Caribbean Sea

Martinique Passage

❸ Sarah Honychurch's labor of love, **D'Auchamps Gardens** is just outside Roseau en route to Trafalgar. Here, marked walkways pass exotic anthuriums, ferns, heliconias, and many other plants. An "honesty box" at the information area has a sign requesting a $2 donation for your walk and another $1 for the pamphlet that shows what's in the garden and where. Of course, Sarah herself may be on hand to take you on a 1-hour tour ($10). *Open daily 9–4.*

❹ **Morne Trois Pitons National Park,** dedicated as a national park in 1975 and named a UNESCO World Heritage Site in 1998, is a 17,000-acre swath of lush, mountainous land in the south-central interior, the Nature Island's crown jewel. Named after one of the highest (4,600 ft) mountains on the island, it covers 9% of Dominica and contains majestic waterfalls, cool mountain lakes, and the world's largest boiling lake. Ferns grow 30 ft tall and wild orchids sprout from trees, sunlight leaks through green canopies, and a gentle mist rises over the jungle floor. The park comprises a number of spectacular lakes and waterfalls amid the lush vegetation—among them are **Middleham Falls, Boeri Lake** and **Freshwater Lake,** and **Wotten Waven Sulphur Springs.** Expect that a visit to the springs and either the lakes or the falls will require about four hours. Hiking guides are available at most trailheads, but your best bet is to arrange a tour before setting out (*see* Hiking, *below*).

The undisputed highlight of the park is **Boiling Lake,** a cauldron of gurgling gray-blue water 70 yards wide and of unknown depth, with water temperatures from 180°F to 197°F. It's believed that the lake is not a volcanic crater but a flooded fumarole—a crack through which gases escape from the molten lava below. The two- to four-hour (one way) hike up to the lake is challenging. On your way you'll traverse the Valley of Desolation, a sight that definitely lives up to its name. Harsh, sulphuric fumes have destroyed virtually all the vegetation in what must once have been a lush forested area. Small hot and cold streams with water of various colors—black, purple, red, orange—web the valley. During this hike, you'll pass rivers where you can refresh yourself with a dip. You'll need attire appropriate for a strenuous hike, a change of dry clothes (wrapped in plastic), and a guide (*see* Hiking, *below*). Note that most full-day hikes to Boiling Lake commence no later than 8:30 AM, so you'll need to plan ahead to make this trip while your ship is in port.

Just beyond the village of Trafalgar (about 15 minutes northeast of Roseau), is the entrance to **Trafalgar Falls.** In the reception facility you can buy park passes and find a guide to take you on a rain forest trek to the twin falls. If you like a little challenge, let your guide take you up the riverbed to the cool pools at the base of the falls. The trek will take about 20 minutes each way.

The **Emerald Pool** is a swirling natural pool into which a 50-ft waterfall splashes. Part of the Morne Trois Pitons National Park, the pool is an easy 20-minute walk from the park's reception facility. Along the forested trail you'll pass exotic flora and several lookout points with views of the Atlantic coast. The Emerald Pool is easily visited from Roseau or Portsmouth and is well matched with a visit to the Carib Indian Territory (*see below*). Expect to set aside about 3 ½ hours for the trip.

⑤ The 3,700 acres of the **Carib Indian Territory,** on the northeast coast of Dominica, were granted in 1903 to the Carib Indians, the first inhabitants of the Caribbean, to establish a reservation. Its generous, shy, proud inhabitants live like most other people in rural Caribbean communities. Many are farmers and fishermen; others are entrepreneurs. Still others are craftspeople whose knowledge of basket weaving, woodcarving, and canoe building has been passed down from one generation to the next for centuries. You can buy exquisitely made Carib baskets at roadside stands. (Note that the prices are ridiculously low considering the high quality of the work and the labor-intensive techniques used to make it; to bargain would be offensive).

Within the territory is **L'Escalier Tête Chien** (Snake's Staircase), a hardened lava flow formation that runs down into the Atlantic. The ocean is particularly fierce here and the shore is full of countless coves and inlets. According to Carib legend, at night the nearby Londonderry Islets metamorphose into canoes to take the spirits of the dead out to sea.

⑥ The **Syndicate Nature Trail** weaves through the Syndicate Estate, a protected site set aside as the habitat of the flying pride of Dominica, the green and purple Sisserou parrot

(*Amazona imperialis*). The Sisserou, which appears on Dominica's flag, is found only on Dominica and is an endangered species. At last count there were only 150–300 of these shy, beautiful birds in the wild. The Jaco or red-necked parrot (*Amazona arausiaca*) is found here in greater numbers, and countless other species of birds and wildlife live here as well. About 40 minutes along the West Coast Road, which runs through three types of forests, you will come to the Syndicate Estate and the 200-acre site of Project Sisserou. The trail is a 20-minute walk; don't forget binoculars.

7 **Indian River** in Portsmouth was a Carib Indian settlement before the colonists drove them into the interior. Wildlife spotting along the mangrove-lined river from a rowboat is a relaxing treat. To arrange such a trip, stop by the visitor center at the mouth of the river and ask someone to recommend a guide. Most boat trips take you up as far as the jungle bar (it's customary to buy your guide a drink, though no one would ever ask you to do so). Tours last one to three hours and cost $15–$30 per person.

8 **Cabrits National Park**—along with Brimstone Hill in St. Kitts, Shirley Heights in Antigua, and Fort Charlotte in St. Vincent—is among the most significant historic sites in the Caribbean. The heart of the park is the Fort Shirley military complex, built by the British between 1770 and 1815. With the help of the Royal Navy and local volunteers, historian Dr. Lennox Honychurch has restored the fort. Onsite there's also a small museum. The herbaceous swamps near the docks are an important site for several species of rare birds and plants, including the white mangrove.

Shopping

Dominicans produce a variety of distinctive handicrafts. Vetiver straw mats, screw pine basketwork, and wood carvings are sold in shops all over the island. Also notable are spices (especially saffron), hot peppers, bay rum, and coconut oil. Café Dominique, the local equivalent of Jamaican Blue Mountain coffee, is an excellent buy, as are Dominican rums, Macoucherie and Soca. Proof that the old ways live on in Dominica can be found in the number of herbal remedies available. One stimulating memento of your visit is rum steeped with Bois Bandé (scientific name *Richeria grandis*), a tree whose bark is reputed to have aphrodisiac properties. Most major supermarkets stock many of these items—try **Brizee's** (Canefield, tel. 767/448–2087) or **Whitchurch** (Kennedy Ave., Roseau, tel. 767/448–2181).

Stores are generally open from 8 until 4 or 5 on weekdays and from 8 to 1 on Saturdays. Most are closed on Sundays. Vendors are almost always out when a ship's in port.

One of the easiest places to pick up a souvenir is the **Old Market Plaza.** Slaves were once sold here, but today it's the scene of happier trading: key rings, magnets, dolls, baskets, handcrafted jewelry, T-shirts, spices, souvenirs, and batiks are available from a select group of entrepreneurs in open-air booths set up on the cobblestones.

For local crafts in Roseau, stop by **Caribana's Iris Dangleben Gallery** (31 Cork St., tel. 767/448–7340), the island's oldest craft shop, which carries only Dominican arts and crafts. The rear of the store showcases fine art by local and visiting artists and is a popular gathering spot for the local artistic community. **The Rainforest Shop** (17 Old St., tel. 767/448–8834) purveys everything from toucan-shape toothbrush holders to doorstops. **The Crazy Banana** (17 Castle St., tel. 767/449–8091) sells Caribbean-made crafts, rums, cigars, and jewelry. **Balizier** (35 Great George St.) is a showroom for the work of Hilroy Fingol, a young artist who specializes in airbrush painting. His mom and sister also stock the store with decorated straw hats, carnival dolls, and island jewelry. In the back room of **Tropicrafts** (Queen Mary St. at Turkey La., tel. 767/448–2747) you can watch women weaving grass mats. The shop also carries arts and crafts from around the Caribbean—local wood carvings, rum, perfumes, and traditional Carib baskets.

Sports

HIKING

The island's best hikes are within **Morne Trois Pitons National Park** (*see* Exploring Dominica, *above*). Guides for hikes to Boiling Lake, Middleham and Trafalgar falls, and Emerald Pool can be arranged through the **Dominica Forestry Division** (tel. 767/448–2401 or 767/448–2638) or the **Dominican Tourist Office** (Dame M. E. Charles Blvd., no phone), which is open weekdays 8–4 and Saturday 9–1. Guides will charge about $10–$30 per person.

Dominica is a paradise for divers and snorkelers. The beaches of the southwest coast are mostly rocks and black sand, but the snorkeling and scuba diving are excellent because of the dramatic underwater walls, sudden drops, and very clear waters. At Scotts Head and Soufrière Bay you'll find some of the world's finest snorkeling and diving. At one spot volcanic vents puff steam into the sea; the experience has been described as "swimming in champagne," so the spot has come to be called "Champagne." For information about excursions, call **Anchorage Dive Centre** (Anchorage Hotel, Castle Comfort, tel. 767/448–2638), **Dive Castaways** (Castaway Beach Hotel, Mero, tel. 767/449–6244), **Dive Dominica** (Castle Comfort Lodge, tel. 767/448–2188), or **Nature Island Dive** (Soufrière, tel. 767/448–8181).

Beaches and River Bathing

On Dominica you'll find mostly black-sand beaches, evidence of the island's volcanic origins, or secluded white- or brown-sand beaches along the northeast coast. The best sand beaches are around Portsmouth, but swimming off the rocky shores has its pleasures, too: the water is deeper and bluer, and the snorkeling is far more interesting. **Picard Beach,** on the northwest coast, is the island's best beach. Great for swimming, windsurfing and snorkeling, it's a 2-mi stretch of brown sand fringed with coconut trees. The beaches of the southwest coast are mostly rocks and black sand.

On an island with 365 rivers, it's not surprising that river swimming is one of the most popular pastimes on Dominica. On the west coast, good bets include the **Macoucherie River** and the **Picard River.** Both are clean, and you can also sunbathe and picnic on their banks.

Dining

There is a 3% restaurant tax added to all bills. Some restaurants include a 10% service charge in the final tab; otherwise tip 10% for good service.

$$ **Papillote Restaurant.** Just outside Anne Jean-Baptiste's stone-and-tile restaurant, you'll find botanical gardens and a bubbling hot-spring pool—just the spot to savor a lethal rum punch. Try the superb Creole fare, for example Anne's traditional flying-fish sandwiches, dasheen puffs, bracing callaloo soup, chicken rain forest (marinated with papaya and wrapped in banana leaves), and, if they're on the menu, succulent freshwater shrimp. *Trafalgar Falls Rd., Roseau (15 min from downtown), tel. 767/448–2287. Reservations essential. AE, D, MC, V.*

$$ La Robe Creole. This one-story stone building is just south of the Old Market Plaza. Retreat into the cozy dining room with wood rafters, ladder-back chairs, and colorful madras tablecloths, and choose from the eclectic menu of Creole cuisine. Callaloo soup, made with dasheen and coconut, is a specialty. Other tasty options include lobster and conch crepes and charcoal-grilled fish. *3 Victoria St., Roseau, tel. 767/448–2896. D, MC, V. Closed Sun.*

$–$$ Callaloo Restaurant. Mrs. Marge Peters, the hostess of this informal eatery, takes pride in age-old cooking traditions and uses only the freshest local produce. (What she does with breadfruit alone—roasted slabs, puffs, creamy velouté, juice, pie—could fill a cookbook.) Lunch specials might include pepper-pot soup, curried conch, or callaloo—fragrant with cumin, lime, clove, and garlic. *66 King George V St., Roseau, tel. 767/448–3386. AE, D, MC, V.*

Grand Cayman

The largest and most populous of the Cayman Islands, Grand Cayman is also one of the most popular cruise destinations in the western Caribbean, largely because it doesn't suffer from the ailments afflicting many larger ports: panhandlers, hasslers, and crime. Instead, the Cayman economy is a study in stability, and residents are renowned for their courteous behavior. Though cacti and scrub fill the dusty landscape, Grand Cayman is a diver's paradise, with pristine waters and a colorful variety of marine life.

Compared with other Caribbean ports, there are fewer things to see on land here; instead, the island's most impressive sights are underwater. Snorkeling, diving, and glass-bottom-boat and submarine rides top every ship's shore-excursion list and can also be arranged at major aquatic shops. Grand Cayman is also famous for the 554 offshore banks in George Town; not surprisingly, the standard of living is high, and nothing is cheap.

Currency

The U.S. dollar is accepted everywhere. The Cayman Island dollar (CI$) is worth about US$1.20. Prices are often quoted in Cayman dollars, so make sure you know which currency you're dealing with. All prices given below are in U.S. dollars unless otherwise indicated.

Telephones

Calling the United States is the same as calling long distance in the States: Just dial 01 followed by the area code and telephone number. To place a credit-card call, dial 110.

Shore Excursions

The following are good choices in Grand Cayman. They may not be offered by all cruise lines. Times and prices are approximate.

UNDERSEA CREATURES

Atlantis **Submarine.** A real submarine offers an exciting view of Grand Cayman's abundant marine life. *1½ hrs. Cost: $79.*

Seaworld Explorer Cruise. A glass-bottom boat takes you on an air-conditioned, narrated voyage where you sit 5 ft below the water's surface and see sunken ships, tropical fish, and coral reefs. *1 hr. Cost: $29.*

Snorkeling Adventure. Novices can take lessons and experienced snorkelers will find adventure on this trip to one or two sites. For a once-in-a-lifetime experience, the Sting Ray City tour is recommended. *2½ hrs. Cost: $34.*

Coming Ashore

Ships anchor in George Town Harbor and tender passengers onto Harbour Drive, the center of the shopping district. A tourist information booth is on the pier, and taxis line up for disembarking passengers. Taxi fares are determined by an elaborate rate structure set by the government, and although they may seem expensive, cabbies rarely try to rip off tourists. Ask to see the chart if you want to check a quoted fare.

Exploring Grand Cayman

You can explore George Town on foot. The small but fascinating **Cayman Islands National Museum,** to the right of the tender landing and just across the street, is well worth visiting if only to see the three-dimensional view of how the island looks above and below the sea. *Tel. 345/949–8368. Admission: CI$5. Open weekdays 9–5, Sat. 10–4.*

On Cardinal Avenue is the **General Post Office,** built in 1939, with strands of decorative colored lights and about 2,000 private mailboxes (island mail is not delivered).

Behind the general post office is **Elizabethan Square,** a complex that houses clothing and souvenir stores. At the corner of Fort and Edward streets, notice the small clock tower dedicated to Britain's King George V and the huge fig tree pruned into an umbrella shape.

The **Old Homestead,** formerly known as the West Bay Pink House, is probably the most photographed home in Grand Cayman. This pink-and-white cottage was built in 1912 of wattle and daub around an ironwood frame. Tours are led by Mac Bothwell, a cheery guide who grew up here. *W. Bay Rd., tel. 345/949–7639. Admission: $5. Open Mon.–Sat. 8–5.*

Near the Old Homestead is the tiny village of **Hell,** which is little more than a patch of incredibly jagged rock formations called ironshore. The big attractions here are a small post office, which sells stamps and postmarks cards from Hell (the postcard of bikini-clad beauties emblazoned "When Hell Freezes Over" gives you the idea), and lots of T-shirt and souvenir shops.

The **Cayman Island Turtle Farm** is the island's most popular attraction. Here you'll see turtles of all ages, from day-old hatchlings to huge 600-pounders that live to be 100. In the adjoining café, sample turtle soup or sandwiches. *W. Bay Rd., tel. 345/949–3893. Admission: $6. Open Mon.–Sat. 8:30–5.*

At **Bodden Town**—the island's original capital—you'll find an old cemetery on the shore side of the road. Graves with A-frame structures are said to contain the remains of pirates. A curio shop serves as the entrance to what's called the Pirate's Caves, partially underground natural formations that are more hokey than spooky.

Queen Elizabeth II Botanic Park is a 65-acre wilderness preserve that showcases the habitats and plants native to the Caymans. Signs identify the flora along the 1½-km-long

TO LITTLE CAYMAN
80 miles

TO

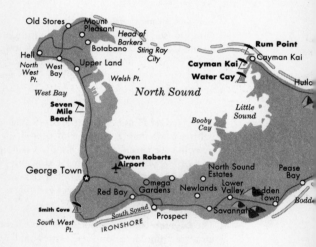

Old Stores

Mount
Pleasant

*Head of
Barkers*

Botabano

*Sting Ray
City*

Rum Point

Cayman Kai

Hell

*North
West
Pt.*

West
Bay

Upper Land

Cayman Kai

Water Cay

Hutlo

West Bay

Welsh Pt.

North Sound

**Seven
Mile
Beach**

*Little
Sound*

*Booby
Cay*

**Owen Roberts
Airport**

George Town

North Sound
Estates

Pease
Bay

Red Bay

Omega
Gardens

Newlands

Lower
Valley

Bodden
Town

Bodde

Smith Cove

South Sound

*South West
Pt.*

IRONSHORE

Prospect

Savannah

KEY

Beaches

TO CAYMAN BRAC
85 miles

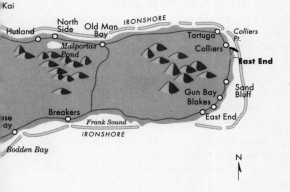

Caribbean Sea

Kai

Hutland

North
Side

Old Man
Bay

IRONSHORE

*Malportas
Pond*

Tortuga

*Colliers
Pt.*

Colliers

East End

Sand
Bluff

Gun Bay
Blakes

East End

Breakers

Frank Sound

IRONSHORE

Bodden Bay

use
ay

N

0			4 miles
0			6 km

(1-mi-long) walking trail. Halfway along the route is a walled compound housing the rare blue iguana—it's found only in remote sections of the islands. *Frank Sound Rd., tel. 345/947–9462. Admission: $3. Open daily 9–6:30.*

The Mastic Reserve and Trail is part of the largest contiguous area of untouched old growth woodland on the island. It passes through black mangrove, abandoned agricultural land, and ancient dry woodlands. The trail is 2 mi long and the guided tour takes about 2½ to 3 hours. Although this is not a rigorous hike, it is a lengthy walking tour—so be sure you're in adequate shape. The tour costs $45 per person. *Off Frank Sound Rd., north side, tel. 345/945–6588. Reservations essential for tours. Open daily 9–5.*

On the way to the East End are the **Blow Holes,** a great photo opportunity as waves crash into the fossilized coral beach, forcing water into caverns and sending geysers shooting up through the ironshore.

Beyond the Blow Holes is the village of **East End,** the first recorded settlement on Grand Cayman. As the highway curves north, you'll come to Queen's View lookout point. There's a monument commemorating the legendary Wreck of the Ten Sails, which took place just offshore.

Pedro St. James Castle is the oldest stone building in the Cayman Islands, estimated to have been built in 1780. Legends linked to it abound, but what is known is that the building was struck by lightning in 1877 and left in ruins until bought by a restaurateur in the 1960s. Gutted once again by fire in 1970, the building was purchased by the government in 1991 and has since undergone extensive renovations. *South Sound Rd., Savannah, tel. 345/947–3329.*

Shopping

Fort Street and Cardinal Avenue are the main shopping streets in George Town. On Cardinal Avenue is Kirk Freeport Plaza, with lots of jewelry shops. The **Tortuga Rum Company** (tel. 345/949–7701) bakes a scrumptious rum cake that's sweet and moist and makes a great souvenir. **Heritage Craft** (tel. 345/945–6041), opposite the National Museum, has a large selection of wind chimes, hammocks, handmade dolls, wood carvings, and local arts. A short drive down South Church Street will take you to **Pure Art** (tel. 345/949–

9133), which has unique local paintings, prints, artsy frames, mugs, and handmade collectibles.

Sports

FISHING

For fishing enthusiasts, Cayman waters are abundant with blue and white marlin, yellowfin tuna, sailfish, dolphinfish, bonefish, and wahoo. If your ship doesn't offer a fishing excursion, about 25 boats are available for charter. Ask at the tourist information booth on the pier.

SCUBA DIVING AND SNORKELING

If you're interested in a diving excursion, contact **Bob Soto's Diving Ltd.** (tel. 345/949–2022 or 800/262–7686), **Don Foster's Dive Grand Cayman** (tel. 345/945–5132 or 800/ 833–4837), and **Parrot's Landing** (tel. 345/949–7884 or 800/ 448–0428). The best snorkeling is off the **Ironshore Reef** (within walking distance of George Town on the west coast) and the north and south coasts, where coral and fish are much more varied and abundant.

Beaches

The west coast, the island's most developed area, is where you'll find the famous **Seven Mile Beach.** This white, pow-dery stretch (actually 5½ mi long) is Grand Cayman's busi-est vacation center, and most of the island's resorts, restaurants, and shopping centers are along this strip. The Holiday Inn rents Aqua Trikes, Paddle Cats, and Banana Rides.

Dining

Many restaurants add a 10%–15% service charge.

$$$ **Lantana's.** Try the American-Caribbean cuisine at this fine eatery, where the decor is as imaginative and authentic as the food, and both are of top quality. Lobster quesadillas, blackened king salmon over cilantro linguine with banana fritters and cranberry relish, incredible roasted garlic soup, and apple pie are favorites from the diverse menu. *Caribbean Club, W. Bay Rd., Seven Mile Beach, tel. 345/947–5595. AE, D, MC, V. No lunch weekends.*

$$ **Cracked Conch by the Sea.** If you visit the Turtle Farm, this restaurant is right next door and worth a visit for lunch. Patio diners will enjoy a panoramic view of the sea. Spe-cialties include conch fritters, conch chowder, spicy Cay-man-style snapper, turtle steak, and other seafood offerings.

A collection of antique diving equipment makes the place something of a diver's museum. *West Bay Rd. near Turtle Bay Farm, tel. 345/947–5217. MC, V.*

$$ Captain Bryan's. For a beer and a bite to eat with a view of the sea, this colorful café is just a few minutes' walk from the tender landing. Ask for a table on the outdoor deck that overlooks the beach and try a Stingray on draft—a British-style, Cayman-brewed pilsner. To get here, make a left as you exit the dock and stroll down Harbor Road (the name of the road changes to North Church Street). *N. Church St. on waterfront, tel. 345/949–6163. AE, MC, V.*

$ Breadfruit Tree Garden. This spot is a favorite with locals, and the price is certainly right. The jerk chicken may just be the best on the island, and the menu also has curry chicken and stewed pork, oxtail, rice and beans, and home-made soups. The interior has an island-country kitsch look with silk roses, white porch swings, straw hats, empty bird cages and fake ivy crawling along the ceiling. It's less than a five-minute cab ride from town. *Eastern Ave., George Town, tel. 345/945–2124. No credit cards.*

Grenada and Carriacou

Nutmeg, cinnamon, cloves, cocoa . . . the aromas fill the air and all memories of Grenada (pronounced gruh-*nay*-da). Only 33½ km (21 mi) long and 19½ km (12 mi) wide, the Isle of Spice is a tropical gem of lush rain forests, white-sand beaches, secluded coves, and exotic flowers.

Until 1983, when the U.S.–Eastern Caribbean intervention catapulted this little nation into the headlines, Grenada was a relatively obscure island hideaway for lovers of fishing, snorkeling, or simply lazing in the sun. Grenada has been back to normal for years. It's a safe and secure vacation spot with friendly, hospitable people and enough good shopping, restaurants, historic sites, and natural wonders to make it a popular port of call. Tourism is growing each year, but the expansion of tourist facilities is carefully controlled. New construction on the beaches must be at least 165 ft back from the high-water mark, and no building can stand taller than a coconut palm. As a result, Grenada continues to retain its distinctly West Indian identity.

Nearby Carriacou (pronounced *car*-ree-a-coo) is visited mostly by sailing ships. Part of the three-island nation of Grenada (Petit Martinique, a tiny island 3 km/2 mi north of Carriacou, is the third), the 21-square-km (13-square-mi) island is 37 km (23 mi) north of the island of Grenada. Carriacou is the largest and southernmost island of the Grenadines, an archipelago of 32 small islands and cays that stretch northward from Grenada to St. Vincent.

The colonial history of Carriacou parallels Grenada's, but the island's small size has restricted its role in the nation's political history. Carriacou is hilly and not lush like Grenada. In fact, it's quite arid in some areas. A chain of hills cuts a wide swath through the center, from Gun Point in the north to Tyrrel Bay in the south. The island's greatest attractions for cruise passengers are diving and snorkeling.

Currency

Grenada uses the Eastern Caribbean (E.C.) dollar. The exchange rate is EC$2.70 to US$1, although taxi drivers, stores, and vendors will frequently calculate at a rate of EC$2.50. U.S. dollars are readily accepted, but always ask which currency is being referenced when asking prices. All prices given below are in U.S. dollars unless otherwise indicated.

Telephones

U.S. and Canadian telephone numbers can be dialed directly. Pay phones and phone cards are available at the welcome center, on the Carenage in St. George's, where cruise-ship passengers come ashore. To place an international call using a major credit card, dial 111; there's no surcharge.

Shore Excursions

The following are good choices in Grenada. They may not be offered by all cruise lines. Times and prices are approximate.

ISLAND SIGHTS

City and Spice Tour. Tour St. George's, then ride north along the spectacular west coast, through small villages and lush greenery. Stop along the way to see how nutmegs are processed. *3 hrs. Cost: $34.*

NATURE TOURS

Spice and Rum Tour. Visit the cottage industries of Grenada, including a nutmeg factory (Grenada is the world's second-largest nutmeg producer), a small soap-and-perfume factory, and a rum factory. You can see how the products are made and, if you wish, purchase samples. *3 hrs. Cost: $34.*

Island Sights and Grand Étang. Tour the capital, then travel north through Grenada's central mountain range to the rain forest, Crater Lake, and Grand Étang National Park. *3¼ hrs. Cost: $38.*

Coming Ashore

Large ships anchor outside St. George's Harbour and tender passengers to the east side of the Carenage, a thoroughfare that surrounds the horseshoe-shape harbor. Smaller ships dock beside the welcome center. You can easily tour the capital on foot, but be prepared to climb up and down steep hills. At the welcome center, you can hire a walking-tour guide ($5 an hour), a taxi to take you around the Carenage to Market Square ($3 each way), or a water taxi across the harbor (50¢ each way).

To explore areas outside St. George, hiring a taxi or arranging a guided tour is more sensible than renting a car. Taxis are plentiful, and fixed rates to popular island destinations are posted at the welcome center. Cab drivers charge $15 per hour; island tours generally cost $40–$55 per person for a full day of sightseeing, including lunch.

Water taxis are the most picturesque way to get from the welcome center to the beach; one-way fare is $5 to Grand Anse, $10 to Morne Rouge. Minibuses are the least expensive (and most crowded) way to travel between St. George's and Grand Anse. Catch one just outside the welcome center, pay EC$1 (37¢), and hold on to your hat!

Exploring Grenada

Numbers in the margin correspond to points of interest on the Grenada and Carriacou map.

ST. GEORGE'S

① **St. George's** is one of the most picturesque towns in the Caribbean. Pastel-painted buildings with orange-tile roofs line the Carenage. Small, rainbow-color houses rise up from the waterfront and disappear into green hills. On weekends, a windjammer is likely to be anchored in the harbor, giving the scene a 19th-century appearance.

The Carenage is the roadway and walkway around the horsehoe-shape harbor and St. George's main thoroughfare. Take a walk from the welcome center all the way around to Ft. George—stopping at small shops along the way or simply taking in the view and the waterfront activity.

Ft. George, built by the French in 1708, rises high above the entrance to the harbor. The first shots were fired from the fort on October 19, 1983, when Prime Minister Maurice Bishop and some of his followers were assassinated in the courtyard. The assassinations, part of a bloody political coup, were among the events that led to the controversial United States invasion of Grenada six days later. The fort now houses Grenada's police headquarters but is open to the public. The 360-degree view from here is magnificent. *Admission free. Open daily during daylight hrs.*

A couple of blocks from the harbor, the **Grenada National Museum** has a small collection of archaeological artifacts and colonial items. You'll find the young Josephine Bonaparte's marble bathtub, old rum-making equipment, and political memorabilia documenting the 1983 intervention. *Young and Monckton Sts., tel. 473/440–3725. Admission: $1. Open weekdays 9–4:30, Sat. 10–1.*

Don't miss **Market Square,** on Granby Street. It's open weekday mornings but really comes alive on Saturday from 8 AM to noon. Vendors sell baskets, spices, clothing, and fresh produce in a colorful, noisy, and generally exciting atmosphere.

THE WEST COAST

② **Concord Falls,** up the Coast Road about 13 km (8 mi) north of St. George's, consists of three beautiful cascades and is a great spot for hiking. There's a small visitors center at the first waterfall; from here it's a 3-km (2-mi) hike through tropical rain forest to get to the others. The farthest one thunders down 65 ft onto huge boulders, creating a natural pool. You should definitely use a guide for this hike, as it can be slippery and tricky in places. Bring your bathing suit during the dry months (January to May),

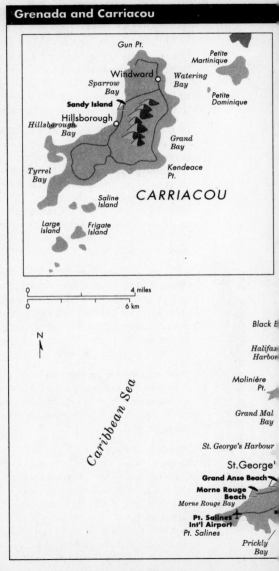

Grenada and Carriacou

Gun Pt.

Petite
Martinique

Windward

Watering
Bay

Sparrow
Bay

Petite
Dominique

Sandy Island

Hillsborough

*Hillsborough
Bay*

Grand
Bay

Kendeace
Pt.

*Tyrrel
Bay*

CARRIACOU

Saline
Island

Large
Island

Frigate
Island

0 — 4 miles
0 — 6 km

N

Black B

Halifax
Harbor

Molinière
Pt.

Grand Mal
Bay

St. George's Harbour

Caribbean Sea

St.George'

Grand Anse Beach

**Morne Rouge
Beach**
Morne Rouge Bay

**Pt. Salines
Int'l Airport**
Pt. Salines

Prickly
Bay

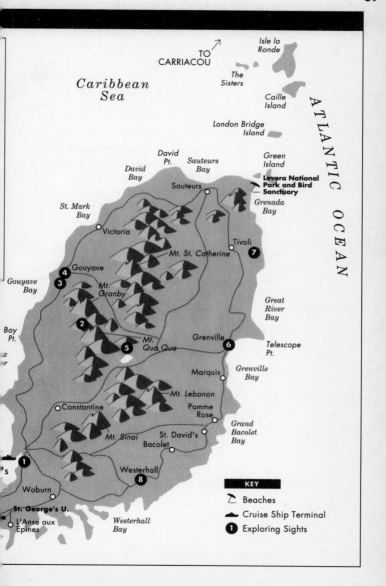

when the currents aren't too strong, and you can step under the cascade. *No phone. Admission: $1. Open daily 9–4.*

③ Dougaldston Spice Estate is a historic plantation that still processes cocoa, nutmeg, mace, cloves, cinnamon, and other spices the old-fashioned way. You'll see the spices laid out on giant rolling trays to dry in the sun. A worker will be happy to explain the process—you can sniff, taste, and buy some spices. *Coast Rd. just south of Gouyave. No phone. Admission: $1. Open weekdays 9–4.*

④ The ½-hour tour of the **Gouyave Nutmeg Processing Co-operative,** in the center of Gouyave, is fragrant and fascinating. The three-story plant turns out 3 million pounds per year of Grenada's most famous export. *Coast Rd., Gouyave, tel. 473/444–8337. Admission: $1. Open weekdays 10–1 and 2–4.*

CENTRAL GRENADA

⑤ In the center of lush, mountainous Grenada is **Grand Etang National Park,** a bird sanctuary and forest reserve where you can fish, hike, and swim. Crater Lake, in an extinct volcano, is a 36-acre expanse of cobalt-blue water 1,740 ft above sea level. *Main Interior Rd., between Grenville and St. George's, tel. 473/440–6160. Admission: $1. Open weekdays 8:30–4.*

⑥ Grenville, on the Atlantic coast and Grenada's second-largest city, retains its historical identity as a French market town; Saturday is market day. The local spice-processing factory, the largest on the island, is open to the public.

⑦ At the rustic **River Antoine Rum Distillery,** you can see rum produced by the same methods used since 1785. The process begins with the crushing of sugarcane from adjacent fields. The result is a potent overproof rum that will knock your socks off. *River Antoine Estate, St. Patrick's, tel. 473/442–7109. Admission: $1. Guided tours daily 9–4.*

⑧ Westerhall, a residential area about 8 km (5 mi) southeast of St. George's, is known for its beautiful villas, gardens, and panoramic views.

GRAND ANSE/SOUTH END

Most of Grenada's resort activity is in or near Grand Anse or the adjacent community of L'Anse aux Epines. There's

In case you want to see the world.

At American Express, we're here to make your journey a smooth one. So we have over 1,700 travel service locations in over 130 countries ready to help. What else would you expect from the world's largest travel agency?

do more

Travel

In case you want to be welcomed there.

We're here to see that you're always welcomed at establishments everywhere. That's why millions of people carry the American Express® Card – for peace of mind, confidence, and security, around the world or just around the corner.

do more

Cards

In case you're running low.

We're here to help with more than 190,000 Express Cash locations around the world. In order to enroll, just call American Express at 1 800 CASH-NOW before you start your vacation.

do more

Express Cash

And in case you'd rather be safe than sorry.

We're here with American Express® Travelers Cheques. They're the safe way to carry money on your vacation, because if they're ever lost or stolen you can get a refund, practically anywhere or anytime. To find the nearest place to buy Travelers Cheques, call 1 800 495-1153. Another way we help you do more.

do more

Travelers Cheques

a small shopping center, too, but beautiful Grand Anse Beach is the main attraction (*see* Beaches, *below*).

Shopping

Spices are a best buy. All kinds are grown and processed in Grenada and cost a fraction of what they command back home in a supermarket. They're available at vendor stalls just outside the welcome center and at the market.

Stores in St. George's are generally open weekdays 8–4 or 4:30, Saturday 8–1. Most are closed on Sunday, though some shops open and vendors appear if ships are in port.

For native handicrafts, **Grenada Craft Centre** (tel. 473/440–9512), on Lagoon Road south of the Carenage, is both a workshop and store. You can watch artisans create jewelry, pottery, batik, wood carvings, baskets, screen-printed T-shirts, and woven items that are all sold in the shop next door. For Caribbean art and antique engravings, visit **Yellow Poui Art Gallery** (tel. 473/444–3001), on Cross Street in St. George's. **Tikal** (Young St., tel. 473/440–2310) is a long-established boutique with exquisite handicrafts, baskets, artwork, jewelry, carvings, batik items, and fashions—both locally made and imported from Africa and Latin America. **Art Fabrik** (9 Young St., tel. 473/440–0568) is a batik studio where you can watch artisans create the designs by painting fabric with hot wax. You can buy batik by the yard or fashioned into clothing and other items.

Sports

GOLF

The **Grenada Golf & Country Club** (tel. 473/444–4128) near Grand Anse has a 9-hole golf course and is open to cruise passengers. Fees are EC$7, and rental clubs are available.

WATER SPORTS

Hotels on Grand Anse Beach have water-sports centers where you can rent small sailboats, Windsurfers, and Sunfish. For scuba diving, contact **Dive Grenada** at Allamanda Beach Resort (tel. 473/444–1092), **Grand Anse Aquatics, Ltd.** at Coyaba Beach Resort (tel. 473/444–1046), or **Sanvics Scuba Watersports** at Renaissance Grenada Resort (tel. 473/444–4371, ext. 638).

For information about diving excursions off Carriacou, try **Carriacou Silver Diving** on Main Street in Hillsborough (tel. 473/443–7882) or **Tanki's Watersport Paradise, Ltd.** on L'Esterre Bay (tel. 473/443–8406).

Beaches

Grenada has 45 white-sand beaches along its 128 km (80 mi) of coastline. All beaches are open to cruise passengers, and some great stretches of sand are just 10 minutes from the dock in St. George's. **Grand Anse Beach,** the most spectacular and most popular, is a gleaming 3-km (2-mi) curve of pure white sand lapped by clear, gentle surf. **Morne Rouge Beach,** a little southwest of Grand Anse, is less crowded and has a reef that's terrific for snorkeling.

On Carriacou, don't pass up a chance to go to **Sandy Island,** just off Hillsborough. It's a narrow spit of white sand with a cluster of palm trees, surrounded by crystal-clear water and a reef for snorkeling—a true deserted isle. Anyone hanging around the jetty with a motorboat will provide transportation for a few dollars.

Dining

Restaurants usually add a 10% service charge to your bill. If not, tip 10%–15% for a job well done.

GRENADA

$$ Coconut Beach, The French Creole Restaurant. Take local seafood, add butter, wine, and Grenadian herbs, and you have excellent French Creole cuisine. Throw in a beautiful setting right on Grand Anse Beach, and this West Indian cottage becomes a delightful spot for lunch. Lobster is prepared in a dozen different ways. *Grand Anse Beach, tel. 473/444–4644. AE, D, MC, V. Closed Tues.*

$ The Nutmeg. Fresh seafood, homemade West Indian dishes, great hamburgers, and the view of the harbor draw residents and visitors alike. *The Carenage, St. George's, tel. 473/440–2539. AE, D, MC, V.*

$ Rudolf's. This busy English-style waterfront pub offers fine West Indian fare—crab back, *lambi* (conch), and delectable nutmeg ice cream—along with fish-and-chips, sandwiches, and burgers. The rum punches are lethal. *The Carenage, St. George's, tel. 473/440–2241. MC, V. Closed Sun.*

$ **Callaloo Restaurant and Bar.** This quaint waterfront restaurant has extraordinary views of Hillsborough Bay and Sandy Island. Excellent seafood dishes are reasonably priced. Be sure to sample the callaloo soup. *Main St., Hillsborough, tel. 473/443–8004. AE, MC, V. Closed Sept.*

Guadeloupe

On a map, Guadeloupe looks like a giant butterfly resting on the sea between Antigua and Dominica. Its two wings—Basse-Terre and Grande-Terre—are the two largest islands in the 1,054-square-km (659-square-mi) Guadeloupe archipelago. The Rivière Salée, a 6-km (4-mi) channel between the Caribbean and the Atlantic, forms the "spine" of the butterfly. A drawbridge connects the two islands.

If you're seeking a resort atmosphere, casinos, and white sandy beaches, your target is Grande-Terre. On the other hand, Basse-Terre's Natural Park, laced with mountain trails and washed by waterfalls and rivers, is a 74,100-acre haven for hikers, nature lovers, and anyone yearning to peer into the steaming crater of an active volcano.

This port of call is one of the least touristy (and least keen on Americans). Guadeloupeans accept visitors, but their economy does not rely on tourism. Pointe-à-Pitre, the port city, is a kaleidoscope of smart boutiques, wholesalers, sidewalk cafés, produce markets, barred and broken-down buildings, little parks, and bazaarlike stores. Though not to everyone's liking, the city has lots of character.

French is the official language, and few locals speak English—although Guadeloupeans are very similar to Parisians in that if you make an attempt at a few French words, they will usually open up. (It's sensible to carry a postcard of the ship with the name of where it's docked written in French.) Like other West Indians, many Guadeloupeans do not appreciate having their photographs taken. Always ask permission first, and don't take a refusal personally. Also, many locals take offense at short shorts or swimwear worn outside bathing areas.

Currency

Legal tender is the French franc, composed of 100 centimes. At press time, the rate was 5.65F to US$1. All prices given below are in U.S. dollars unless otherwise indicated.

Telephones

To call the United States from Guadeloupe, dial 001-191, the area code, and the local number. For calls within Guadeloupe, dial the six-digit number.

Shore Excursions

The following is a good choice in Guadeloupe. It may not be offered by all cruise lines. Times and prices are approximate.

ISLAND TOUR

Pointe-à-Pitre/Island Drive. Explore both of Guadeloupe's islands—Grande-Terre and Basse-Terre. The tour includes a walk through the lush national park and a stop at a rum factory. If you're not going to explore the island on your own, this tour is highly recommended. *3 hrs. Cost: $40.*

Coming Ashore

Ships dock at the Maritime Terminal of Centre St-John Perse in downtown Pointe-à-Pitre, about a block from the shopping district. To get to the tourist information office, walk along the quay for about five minutes to the Place de la Victoire. The office is across the road at the top of the section of the harbor, called La Darse. There's also a small information booth in the terminal, a branch of the main office.

The most interesting parts of Pointe-à-Pitre, with markets, pastry shops, and modern buildings, is compact and easy to see on foot. If you want to use a taxi driver as a guide, make sure you speak a common language. Taxi fares (more expensive here than on other islands) are regulated by the government and posted at taxi stands. If your French is good, you can call for a cab (tel. 590/82–21–21, 590/83–90–00, or 590/20–74–74). Tip drivers 10%.

Exploring Guadeloupe

Numbers in the margin correspond to points of interest on the Guadeloupe map.

❶ Pointe-à-Pitre, a city of some 100,000 people, lies almost on the "backbone" of the butterfly, near the bridge that crosses the Salée River. With its narrow streets, honking horns, and traffic jams, it's pulsing with life.

The **Musée St-John Perse** is dedicated to the Guadeloupean poet who won the 1960 Nobel Prize in literature. Inside the restored colonial house is a complete collection of his poetry. *Corner of rues Noizières and Achille René-Boisneuf, tel. 590/90–07–92. Admission: 10F. Open Thurs.–Tues. 8:30–12:30 and 2:30–5:30.*

In the cacophonous, colorful **marketplace,** locals bargain for vibrant papayas, breadfruit, christophenes, and tomatoes. Saturday mornings are particularly boisterous. *Between rues St-John Perse, Fré-bault, Schoelcher, and Peynier.*

The **Musée Schoelcher** honors the memory of Victor Schoelcher, the 19th-century Alsatian abolitionist who fought slavery in the French West Indies. Exhibits trace his life and work. *24 rue Peynier, tel. 509/82–08–04. Admission: 10F. Open weekdays 8:30–11:30 and 2–5.*

Place de la Victoire, surrounded by wood buildings with balconies and shutters and lined with sidewalk cafés, was named in honor of Victor Hugues's 1794 victory over the British. During the French Revolution a guillotine here lopped off the heads of many an aristocrat.

The imposing **Cathedral of St. Peter and St. Paul** has survived havoc-wreaking earthquakes and hurricanes. Note the lovely stained-glass windows. *Rue Alexandre Isaac.*

BASSE-TERRE

❷ **La Marina,** between Bas-du-Fort and Pointe-à-Pitre, is a 10-minute cab ride from the cruise-ship terminal. The lively venue comprises a dozen restaurants, bar lounges, and shops around the quay, as well as an aquarium housing a thousand different Caribbean sea creatures. Sailboats and motorboats can be rented here, and excursions depart for the mangroves. The Syndicat d'Initiative (tourist bureau) here is very helpful; it's closed from noon to 2 every day.

High adventure can be yours on a drive across Basse-Terre ❸ to the **Parc National de la Guadeloupe.** For the ecologically minded, this is the place to visit. The park is bisected by the Route de la Traversée (Route D23), a 26-km (16-mi) paved road lined with masses of thick tree ferns, shrubs,

96

Guadeloupe

KEY

Beaches

Cruise Ship Terminal

1 Exploring Sights

La Pointe de la Grande Vigie

borde

and

N6

D122

Campêche

N8

Gros-Cap

Beauport

Anse de la
Savane Brûlée

Les Mangles

N6

D120

Canal
tit-Canal

Baie du
Nord Ouest

urg

Morne-à-l'Eau

N5

Le Moule

N5

N7

GRANDE-TERRE

abrun du Sud

Jabrun
du Nord

Anse á la
Baie

Abymes

ôle Caraïbes
nternational
irport

Tarare

Pte. des
Châteaux

1

St-François

2

Anse
Kahouanne

Gosier

Ste-Anne

**Caravelle
Beach**

Ilet du Gosier

ATLANTIC OCEAN

e

Marie

sterre-
Eau

Grosse Pte.

Vieux Fort

Anse
Chapelle

Baie de
St. Louis

Saint
Louis

Borée

Anse
Ballet

**Aérodrome de
Marie-Galante**

Marie-Galante

Capesterre

aut

Grand-Bourg

Petit-Anse

awen

Pte. Des Basses

N

flowers, tall trees, and green plantains. If you plan to do any exploring, wear rubber-sole shoes and pack a picnic lunch as well as both a swimsuit and a sweater. Once you've reached the coast, head north on Route N2 toward Grand Anse. The road twists and turns up steep hills smothered in tropical vegetation, skirts deep blue bays, and drops to colorful little seaside towns. Constantly changing light, towering clouds, and frequent rainbows add to the beauty.

Shopping

For serious shopping in Pointe-à-Pitre, browse the boutiques and stores along rue Schoelcher, rue Frébault, and rue Noizières. The market square and stalls of La Darse are filled mostly with vegetables, fruits, and housewares, but you will find some straw hats and dolls.

There are dozens of shops in and around the cruise-ship terminal, Centre St-John Perse. Many stores here offer a 20% discount on luxury items purchased with traveler's checks or major credit cards. You can find good buys on anything French—perfume, crystal, wine, cosmetics, and scarves. As for local handcrafted items, you'll see a lot of junk, but you can also find island dolls dressed in madras, finely woven straw baskets and hats, *salako* hats made of split bamboo, madras table linens, and wood carvings.

The following shops are all in Pointe-à-Pitre: For Baccarat, Lalique, Porcelaine de Paris, Limoges, and other upscale tableware, check **Rosebleu** (5 rue Frébault, tel. 590/82–93–43). Guadeloupe's exclusive purveyor of Orlane, Stendhal, and Germaine Monteil is **Vendôme** (8–10 rue Frébault, tel. 590/83–42–44). The largest selection of perfumes is at **Phoenicia** (8 rue Frébault, tel. 590/83–50–36). You many also want to try **Au Bonheur des Dames** (49 rue Frébault, tel. 590/82–00–30).

Other shopping can be found in Ste-Anne. **La Case à Soie** (tel. 590/88–11–31) creates flowing silk dresses and scarves.

Sports

FISHING

Contact **Caraibe Peche** (Marina Bas-du-Fort, tel. 590/90–97–51), **Fishing Club Antilles** (Bouillante, tel. 590/98–70–10), or **Le Rocher de Malendure** (Pigeon, Bouillante, tel. 590/98–28–84).

GOLF

Golf Municipal Saint-François (St-François, tel. 590/88–41–87) has an 18-hole Robert Trent Jones–designed course, an English-speaking pro, and electric carts for rent.

HIKING

Basse-Terre's **Parc National** is abundant with trails, many of which should be attempted only with an experienced guide. Before heading out, pick up a *Guide to the National Park* from the tourist office (*see* Coming Ashore, *above*), which rates the hiking trails according to difficulty. (Note: The majority of mountain trails are in the southern half.) If you want a light hike, head for the **Cascade aux Ecrevisses.** Crayfish Falls is one of the most popular spots on the island. The marked trail (it can be muddy and slippery) leads to the splendid waterfall dashing down into the Corossol River—a good place for a dip.

Guided hikes for up to 12 people are arranged by **Organisation des Guides de Montagne de la Caraïbe** (Maison Forestière, Matouba, tel. 590/94–29–11) or by the **Office de Tourisme de Basse-Terre** (tel. 590/82–24–83). The acknowledged pros in the private sector are **Parfum d'Aventure** (1 Roche Blonval, St. Francois, tel. 590/88–47–62) or **Sport d'Av** (tel. 590/32–58–41), both of which offer everything from four-wheel-drive safaris to sea-kayaking, hiking, and white-water canoeing trips.

HORSEBACK RIDING

La Manade (Saint-Claude, tel. 590/81–52–21) on Basse-Terre offers half- or full-day rides through the rain forest.

WATER SPORTS

Windsurfing, waterskiing, and sailing are available at almost all beachfront hotels. The main windsurfing center is at the **UCPA** hotel club (tel. 590/88–64–80) in St-François. You can also rent equipment at **Holywind** (Résidence Canella Beach, Pointe de la Verdure, Gosier, tel. 590/90–44–00). For diving, head to Basse-Terre. The **Nautilus Club** (Plage de Malendure, tel. 590/98–89–08) is one of the island's top scuba operations and offers snorkeling trips to Pigeon Island, as well as glass-bottom-boat trips.

Beaches

Some of the island's best beaches lie on the south coast of Grande-Terre from Ste-Anne to Pointe des Châteaux. For $5–$10 per person, hotels allow nonguests to use changing facilities, towels, and beach chairs. **Caravelle Beach,** just outside Ste-Anne, is one of the longest and prettiest stretches of sand. Protected by reefs, it's a fine place to snorkel, and you can rent water-sports gear from Club Med. **Raisin-Clairs,** just outside St-François, offers windsurfing, waterskiing, sailing, and other activities, with rentals arranged through the Méridien Hotel. **Tarare** is a secluded cove close to the tip of Pointe des Châteaux, where locals tan in the buff. There are several secluded coves around **Pointe des Châteaux,** where the Atlantic and Caribbean waters meet and crash against huge rocks, sculpting them into castlelike shapes. **La Grande Anse,** just outside Deshaies on the northwest coast of Basse-Terre, is a secluded beach of soft, beige sand sheltered by palms.

Dining

Restaurants are required to include a 15% service charge in the menu price. No additional gratuity is necessary.

$$$ **Le Côte Jardin.** This plant-filled restaurant is in the bustling marina. The menu of haute French Creole cuisine lists dishes that range from basic lamb Provençal to more exotic *escargots de la mer* (sea snails) with garlic butter. It's busy at lunch, so make sure you reserve a table. *La Marina, Bas-Du-Fort, tel. 590/90–91–28. AE, MC, V.*

$–$$ **Le Karacoli.** If you want to make a day out of it, aim for this charming beachfront restaurant. From your table on the terrace, all you'll hear will be the splash of the waves and the rustling of coconut palms. The food is good Creole fare—such as *boudin* (blood sausage) or goat *colombo* (curry)—as well as the usual seafood dishes. For dessert, try the banana flambé, heavily perfumed with rum. *Grande-Anse, north of Deshaies, tel. 590/28–41–17. MC, V. No dinner.*

Jamaica

The third-largest island in the Caribbean, the English-speaking nation of Jamaica enjoys considerable self-sufficiency thanks to tourism, agriculture, and mining. Its physical attractions include jungle-covered mountains, clear waterfalls, and unforgettable beaches, yet the country's greatest resource may be its people. Although 95% of Jamaicans trace their bloodlines to Africa, their national origins also lie in Great Britain, the Middle East, India, China, Germany, Portugal, and South America, as well as in many other islands in the Caribbean. Their cultural life is a rich one—the music, art, and cuisine of Jamaica are vibrant with a spirit easy to sense but as hard to describe as the rhythms of reggae or the streetwise patois.

Don't let Jamaica's beauty cause you to relax the good sense you would use at home. Resist the promise of adventure should any odd character offer to show you the "real" Jamaica. Jamaica on the beaten track is wonderful enough, so don't take chances by wandering too far off it.

Currency

Currency-exchange booths are set up on the docks at Montego Bay and Ocho Rios whenever a ship is in port. The U.S. dollar is accepted virtually everywhere, but change will be made in Jamaican dollars. At press time the exchange rate was J$36 to US$1. All prices given below are in U.S. dollars unless otherwise indicated.

Telephones

Direct telephone services are available in communication stations at the ports. Because of recent fraud problems, some U.S. phone companies (such as MCI) will not accept credit card calls placed from Jamaica. Phones take only Jamaican phone cards, available from kiosks or variety shops.

Shore Excursions

The following are good choices in Jamaica. They may not be offered by all cruise lines. Times and prices are approximate.

NATURAL BEAUTY

Prospect Plantation and Dunn's River Falls. Visit the beautiful gardens of Prospect Plantation, with their bananas, cocoa, coffee, sugarcane, orchids, and other tropical foliage. Then stop at Dunn's River Falls to crawl and climb through the cool water. *4 hrs. Cost: $44.*

Rafting on the Martha Brae River. Glide down this pristine river in a 30-ft, two-seat bamboo raft, admiring the verdant plant life along the river's banks. *5 hrs. Cost: $54.*

Coming Ashore

IN MONTEGO BAY

Many ships use Montego Bay (nicknamed "MoBay"), 108 km (67 mi) to the west of Ocho Rios, as their Jamaican port of call. The cruise port in Montego Bay is a $10 taxi ride from town. There's one shopping center within walking distance of the Montego Bay docks. The Jamaica Tourist Board office is about 5½ km (3½ mi) away on Gloucester Avenue on Doctor's Cave Beach.

IN OCHO RIOS

Most cruise ships dock at this port on Jamaica's north coast, near Dunn's River Falls. Less than 1½ km (1 mi) from the Ocho Rios pier are the Taj Mahal Duty Free Shopping Center and the Ocean Village Shopping Center, where the Jamaica Tourist Board maintains an office. Getting anywhere else in Ocho Rios will require a taxi.

Some of Jamaica's taxis are metered; rates are per car, not per passenger. You can flag cabs on the street. All licensed and properly insured taxis display red Public Passenger Vehicle (PPV) plates. Licensed minivans also bear the red PPV plates. If you hire a taxi driver as a tour guide, be sure to agree on a price before the vehicle is put into gear.

Exploring Jamaica

MONTEGO BAY

The outstanding tour of **Barnett Estates** is led by a charming guide in period costume. The Kerr-Jarrett family has held the land here for 11 generations and still grows coconut, mango, and sugarcane on 3,000 acres. *Granville Main Rd., tel. 876/952–2382. Admission: $10. Open daily 9:30–10 (great house); tours daily 11–6.*

Greenwood Great House, 24 km (15 mi) east of Montego Bay, has no spooky legend to titillate visitors, but it evokes the life on a sugar plantation much more forcefully than does Rose Hall (*see below*). The Barrett family, from which poet Elizabeth Barrett Browning descended, once owned all the land from Rose Hall to Falmouth and built this and several other great houses on it. Highlights of Greenwood include oil paintings of the Barrett family, china made for them by Wedgwood, a library filled with rare books, antique furniture, and exotic musical instruments. *Tel. 876/953–1077. Admission: $10. Open daily 9–6.*

One of the most popular excursions in Jamaica is rafting on the **Martha Brae River** (tel. 876/952–0889 for reservations), a gentle waterway with the romance of a tropical wilderness. Wear your swimsuit for a plunge at the halfway point of the 5-km (3-mi) river run. The ride costs less than $40 for two people.

Rose Hall Great House, perhaps the most impressive in the West Indies in the 1700s, enjoys its popularity less for its architecture than for the legend surrounding its second mistress. The story of Annie Palmer—credited with murdering three husbands and a plantation overseer who was her lover—is told in a novel sold everywhere in Jamaica: *The White Witch of Rose Hall.* The great house is east of Montego Bay, across from the Rose Hall resorts. *Tel. 876/953–2323. Admission: $15. Open daily 9–6.*

OCHO RIOS

Dunn's River Falls is 600 ft of cold, clear, mountain water splashing over a series of stone steps to the warm Caribbean. Don a swimsuit, climb the slippery steps, take the hand of the person ahead of you, and trust that the chain of hands and bodies leads to an experienced guide. The climb leaders are personable, reeling off bits of local lore while telling you where to step. Take a towel and wear tennis shoes. *Off A–1, between St. Ann's and Ocho Rios, tel. 876/974–2857. Admission: $6. Open daily 9–5.*

The tour of **Prospect Plantation** is the best of several offerings that delve into the island's former agricultural lifestyle. It's not just for specialists; virtually everyone enjoys the beautiful views over the White River Gorge and the tour by jitney through a plantation with exotic fruits and tropical trees. Horseback riding through 1,000 acres is available, with one hour's notice, for about $20 per hour. *Tel. 876/994–1373. Admission: $12. Open daily 8–5. Tours Mon.–Sat. 10:30, 2, and 3:30; Sun. 11, 1:30, and 3:30.*

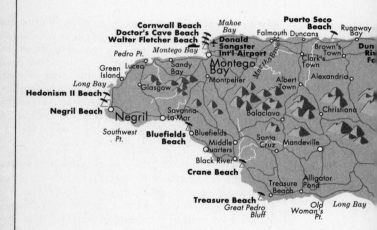

Cornwall Beach
Doctor's Cave Beach
Walter Fletcher Beach

Mahoe Bay

Puerto Seco Beach

Falmouth Duncans

Runaway Bay

Donald Sangster Int'l Airport

Montego Bay

Clark's Town

Brown's Town

Dun Riv Fa

Pedro Pt.

Montego Bay

Green Island

Lucea

Sandy Bay

Montpelier

Albert Town

Alexandria

Long Bay

Hedonism II Beach

Glasgow

Martha Brae

Negril Beach

Negril

Savanna-La-Mar

Balaclava

Christiana

Southwest Pt.

Bluefields Beach

Bluefields

Middle Quarters

Santa Cruz

Mandeville

Black River

Crane Beach

Treasure Beach

Alligator Pond

Treasure Beach

Great Pedro Bluff

Old Woman's Pt.

Long Bay

N

0   10 miles

0   15 km

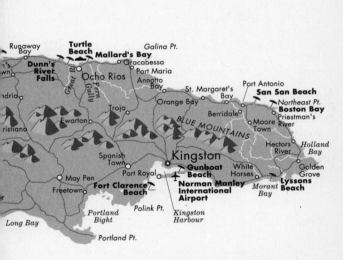

Runaway
Bay
**Turtle
Beach**
Galina Pt.
**Dunn's
River
Falls**
Mallard's Bay
Oracabessa
n's
wn
Port Maria
andria
Ocho Rios
Great Rd.
Fern Gully
Annotto
Bay
St. Margaret's
Bay
Port Antonio
San San Beach
Troja
Orange Bay
Northeast Pt.
Boston Bay
Berridale
Priestman's
River
ristiana
Ewarton
BLUE MOUNTAINS
Moore
Town
Spanish
Town
Hectors
River
Holland
Bay
Kingston
May Pen
Port Royal
**Gunboat
Beach**
White
Horses
Golden
Grove
Freetown
**Fort Clarence
Beach**
**Norman Manley
International
Airport**
Morant
Bay
**Lyssons
Beach**
Portland
Bight
Polink Pt.
Kingston
Harbour
Long Bay
Portland Pt.

Caribbean Sea

KEY
⋝ Beaches
⏵ Cruise Ship Terminal

Shopping

Jamaican artisans express themselves in silk-screening, wood carvings, resort wear, hand-loomed fabrics, and paintings. Jamaican rum makes a great gift, as do Tia Maria (Jamaica's famous coffee liqueur) and Blue Mountain coffee.

Before visiting the crafts markets in Montego Bay and Ocho Rios, consider how much tolerance you have for pandemonium and price haggling. If you're looking to spend money, head for City Centre Plaza, Half Moon Village, Holiday Inn Shopping Centre, Montego Bay Shopping Center, St. James's Place, or Westgate Plaza in Montego Bay; in Ocho Rios, Pineapple Place, Ocean Village, the Taj Mahal, Coconut Grove, and Island Plaza. Some cruise lines run shore excursions that focus on shopping.

For Jamaican and Haitian paintings, head for the **Gallery of West Indian Art** (1 Orange La., Montego Bay, tel. 876/952–4547). A corner of the gallery is devoted to hand-turned pottery and beautifully carved birds and jungle animals. Eight kilometers (6 miles) east of the docks in Ocho Rios is **Harmony Hall** (tel. 876/975–4222), a huge house that has been converted into an art gallery, restaurant, and bar. Wares here include carved items, ceramics, antiques, books, jewelry, fudge, spices, and Blue Mountain coffee.

Sports

GOLF

The best courses are at the **Half Moon Golf, Tennis, and Beach Club** (tel. 876/953–3105), **Ironshore** (tel. 876/953–2800), and **Tryall Golf, Tennis, and Beach Club** (tel. 876/956–5681) in Montego Bay; **Breezes Golf and Beach Resort** in Runaway Bay (tel. 876/973–7319); and **Sandals Golf and Country Club** (tel. 876/975– 0119) in Ocho Rios. Rates range from $50 to $80 for 18 holes at the Ocho Rios and MoBay courses to $110 at Half Moon.

HORSEBACK RIDING

Chukka Cove (St. Ann, tel. 876/972–2506), near Ocho Rios, is the best equestrian facility in the English-speaking Caribbean. Riding is also available at **Prospect Plantation** (Ocho Rios, tel. 876/994–1058) and **Rocky Point Stables** (Half Moon Club, Montego Bay, tel. 876/953–2286).

Beaches

Doctor's Cave Beach at Montego Bay is getting crowded: the 8-km (5-mi) stretch of sugary sand has been spotlighted in so many travel articles and brochures that it's no secret to anyone anymore. On the bright side, it has changing rooms and food vendors. Two other popular beaches near Montego Bay are **Cornwall Beach,** farther up the coast, which has food and drink options and a water-sports concession, and **Walter Fletcher Beach,** on the bay near the center of town. Fletcher offers protection from the surf on a windy day; the unusually calm waters make it good for children.

In Ocho Rios the busiest beach is **Turtle Beach,** not far from the cruise terminal. Several large resorts line the water, but the beach is public, so cruise passengers can enjoy beach bars and grills and water-sports centers.

Dining

Many restaurants add a 10% service charge to the bill. Otherwise, a tip of 10%–20% is customary.

$$–$$$ **Almond Tree.** This very popular restaurant offers a blend of Jamaican and European cuisines. The swinging rope chairs on the terrace bar and the tables perched above a Caribbean cove are great fun. *83 Main St., Ocho Rios, tel. 876/974–2813. Reservations essential. AE, DC, MC, V.*

$$–$$$ **Sugar Mill.** One of the finest restaurants in Jamaica, the Sugar Mill serves seafood with flair on a terrace. Caribbean specialties, steak, and lobster are usually offered in a pungent sauce that blends Dijon mustard with Jamaica's own Pickapeppa. *Half Moon Club, 7 mi east of Montego Bay, tel. 876/953–2228. Reservations essential. AE, MC, V.*

$–$$ **Evita's.** The setting is sensational: an 1860s gingerbread house high on a hill overlooking Ocho Rios Bay (but also convenient from Montego Bay). More than 30 kinds of pasta are served, ranging from lasagna Rastafari (vegetarian) and fiery jerk spaghetti to *rotelle colombo* (crabmeat with white sauce and noodles). *Mantalent Inn, Eden Bower Rd., Ocho Rios, tel. 876/974–2333. AE, MC, V.*

$–$$ **The Native.** This open-air stone terrace, shaded by a large poinciana tree, specializes in Jamaican and international dishes. To go native, start with smoked marlin, move on to the *boonoonoonoos* platter (a sampler of local dishes), and round out the meal with coconut pie or *duckanoo* (a

sweet dumpling of cornmeal, coconut, and banana wrapped
in a banana leaf and steamed). *29 Gloucester Ave., Montego Bay, tel. 876/979–2769. AE, MC, V.*

$ **Ocho Rios Village Jerk Centre.** This blue-canopied, open-air
eatery is a good place to park yourself for frosty Red Stripe
beer and fiery jerk pork, chicken, or seafood. Milder barbecued meats also turn up on the menu. *DaCosta Dr., Ocho
Rios, tel. 876/974–2549. MC, V.*

Key West

The southernmost city in the Continental United States
was originally a Spanish possession. Along with the rest of
Florida, Key West became part of American territory in 1821.
In the late 19th century, Key West was Florida's wealthi-
est city per capita. The locals made their fortunes from
"wrecking"—rescuing people and salvaging cargo from
ships that foundered on nearby reefs. Cigar making, fishing, shrimping, and sponge gathering also became important industries.

Capital of the self-proclaimed "Conch Republic," Key
West today makes for a unique port of call for the 10 or
so ships that visit each week. A genuinely American town,
it nevertheless exudes the relaxed atmosphere and pace of
a typical Caribbean island. Major attractions for cruise passengers are the home of the Conch Republic's most famous
citizen, Ernest Hemingway; the birthplace of now-de-
parted Pan American World Airways; and, if your cruise
ship stays in port late enough, the island's renowned sunset celebrations.

Currency
The U.S. dollar is the only currency accepted in Key West.

Telephones
Public phones are found at the pier and on street corners.
Local calls from most public phones cost 35¢.

Shore Excursions
The following are good choices in Key West. They may not
be offered by all cruise lines. Times and prices are approximate.

ISLAND SIGHTS

Historic Homes Walking Tour. You'll see the Harry S. Truman Little White House, Donkey Milk House, and the Audubon House and Gardens on a short guided stroll through the historic district. *2 hrs. Cost: $29.*

UNDERSEA CREATURES

Reef Snorkeling. The last living coral reefs in Continental America are your destination. Changing facilities, snorkeling gear, and beverages are included. *3 hrs. Cost: $40.*

Coming Ashore

Cruise ships dock at Mallory Square or near the Truman Annex. Both are within walking distance of Duval and Whitehead streets, the two main tourist thoroughfares. For maps and other tourism information, the Chamber of Commerce (402 Wall St., tel. 305/294–2587 or 800/527–8539) is just off Mallory Square.

Because Key West is so easily explored on foot, there is rarely a need to hire a cab. If you plan to venture beyond the main tourist district, a fun way to get around is by bicycle or scooter. Key West is a cycling town. In fact, there are so many bikes around that cyclists must watch out for one another as much as for cars. Try renting from **Keys Moped & Scooter** (tel. 305/294–0399) or **Moped Hospital** (tel. 305/296–3344); both can be found on Truman Avenue. Bike rentals begin at $4 for the day, scooters begin at $14 for three hours. All rentals require a deposit on a credit card.

Two other ways to get around Key West are the **Conch Tour Train** (tel. 305/294–5161) and the **Old Town Trolley** (tel. 305/296–6688). The train provides a 90-minute, narrated tour of Key West that covers 14 mi (22 km) of island sights. Board at the Front Street Depot every half hour from 9 AM to 4:30 PM. The price is $15. The trackless trolley runs 90-minute, narrated tours of Key West. You may get off at any of 12 stops and reboard later. The price is $18.

Exploring Key West

Numbers in the margin correspond to points of interest on the Key West map.

❶ **Mallory Square** is named for Stephen Mallory, secretary of the Confederate Navy, who later owned the Mallory

Key West

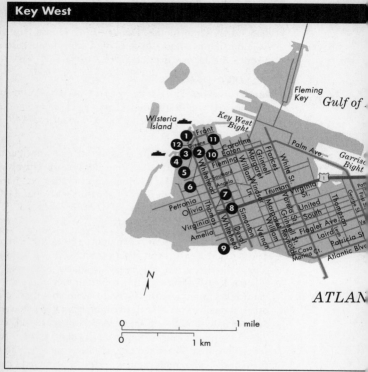

Wisteria Island

Key West Bight

Fleming Key

Gulf of

Garriso Bight

ATLAN

N

0 _____ 1 mile
0 _____ 1 km

Audubon House
and Gardens, **5**

Hemingway
House, **7**

Historic Seaport
at Key West
Bight, **12**

Key West
Aquarium, **2**

Lighthouse
Museum, **8**

Mallory
Square, **1**

Mel Fisher
Maritime
Heritage Society
Museum, **3**

Old City
Hall, **11**

Southernmost
Point, **9**

301 Whitehead
Street, **6**

Truman
Annex, **4**

Wrecker's
Museum, **10**

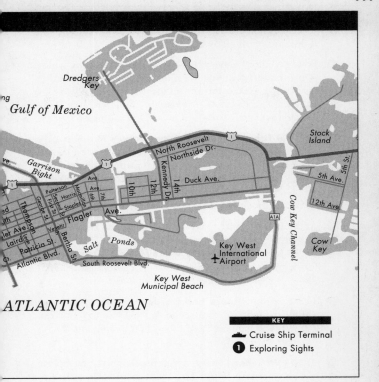

Dredgers Key

Gulf of Mexico

Stock Island

Garrison Bight

North Roosevelt
Northside Dr.

5th St.

5th Ave.

Duck Ave.

12th Ave.

Cow Key Channel

Cow Key

Patterson
Harris
Staples

Flagler Ave.

Salt Ponds

Key West
International
Airport

South Roosevelt Blvd.

Key West
Municipal Beach

ATLANTIC OCEAN

Thompson
George St.
First St.
Venetia

Patricia St.
Bertha St.
Atlantic Blvd.

Laird

10th
12th
14th
Kennedy Dr.

7th
6th

Ave.
Ave.

KEY

Cruise Ship Terminal

1 Exploring Sights

Steamship Line. On nearby Mallory Dock, a nightly sunset celebration draws street performers, food vendors, and thousands of onlookers.

② Facing Mallory Square is the **Key West Aquarium,** which houses hundreds of brightly colored tropical fish and other fascinating sea creatures from local waters. *1 Whitehead St., tel. 305/296– 2051. Admission: $8. Open daily 10–6; guided tours and shark feeding at 11, 1, 3, and 4:30.*

③ The **Mel Fisher Maritime Heritage Society Museum** symbolizes Key West's salvaging past. On display are gold and silver bars, coins, jewelry, and other artifacts recovered in 1985 from two Spanish treasure ships that foundered in 1622. *200 Greene St., tel. 305/294–2633. Admission: $6.50. Open daily 9:30–5:30; last video at 4:30.*

④ At the end of Front Street, the **Truman Annex** is a 103-acre former military parade ground and barracks. Also here is the Harry S. Truman Little White House Museum, in the former president's vacation home. *111 Front St., tel. 305/ 294–9911. Admission: $7.50. Open daily 9–5.*

⑤ The **Audubon House and Gardens** commemorate ornithologist John James Audubon's 1832 visit to Key West. *205 Whitehead St., tel. 305/294–2116. Admission: $7.50. Open daily 9:30–5.*

⑥ At **301 Whitehead Street,** a sign proclaims the birthplace of Pan American World Airways, the first U.S. airline to operate scheduled international air service. The inaugural flight took off from Key West on October 28, 1927.

⑦ Built in 1851, **Hemingway House** was the first dwelling in Key West to have running water and a fireplace. Ernest Hemingway bought the place in 1931 and wrote eight books here. Descendants of Hemingway's cats still inhabit the grounds. Tours begin every 10 minutes. *907 Whitehead St., tel. 305/294–1575. Admission: $6.50. Open daily 9–5.*

Up the block from Hemingway House and across the street, **⑧** behind a white picket fence, is the **Lighthouse Museum,** a 92-ft lighthouse built in 1847 and an adjacent 1848 clapboard house where the keeper lived. You can climb the 88 steps to the top for a spectacular view of the island. *938*

Whitehead St., tel. 305/294–0012. Admission: $6. Open daily 9:30–5, last admission 4:30.

At the foot of Whitehead Street, a huge concrete marker proclaims this spot to be the **Southernmost Point** in the United States. Turn left on South Street. To your right are two dwellings that both claim to be the Southernmost House. Take a right onto Duval Street, which ends at the Atlantic Ocean, and you will be at the Southernmost Beach.

The **Wrecker's Museum** is said to be the oldest house in Key West. It was built in 1829 as the home of Francis Watlington, a sea captain and wrecker. It now contains 18th- and 19th-century period furnishings. *322 Duval St., tel. 305/294–9502. Admission: $4. Open daily 10–4.*

For a look at Key West as it was, visit the restored **Old City Hall.** Inside is a permanent exhibit of Old Key West photographs dating back to 1845. *510 Greene St.*

The newly restored **Historic Seaport at Key West Bight** covers 8½ acres of historic waterfront, bringing together about 100 lively restaurants, stores, bait shops, docks, a marina, wedding chapel, the Waterfront Market, rowing club, dive shops, and open-air bars like the Schooner Wharf (*see* Pub Crawling, *below*). It's linked by the 2-mi waterfront Harborwalk.

The **Reef Relief Environmental Center,** just a couple of doors down from the Schooner Wharf bar, has videos, displays, and free information about the coral reef. *201 William St., tel. 305/294–3100. Open daily 9–5.*

Shopping

Passengers looking for T-shirts, trinkets, and other souvenirs will find them along Duval Street and around the cruise-ship piers. **Fast Buck Freddie's** (500 Duval St., tel. 305/294–2007) is an unusual department store with imaginative merchandise and tropical-themed furniture and clothing. The **Paradise Gift Shop** (430 Duval St., tel. 305/292–8948) is noteworthy for its collection of flamingo items. **Jimmy Buffett's Margaritaville** (500 Duval St., tel. 305/296–3070) sells the music and books of the eponymous singer as well as active wear, housewares, and gadgets with the Buffett insignia. **Key West Island Bookstore** (513 Fleming St., tel.

305/294–2904) is the literary bookstore for the large Key
West writers' community. **Lucky Street Gallery** (1120 White
St., tel. 305/294–3973) carries the work of Keys artists.

Sports

FISHING AND BOATING

The *Discovery* (tel. 305/293–0099) and the *Pride of Key West*
(tel. 305/296–6293) are two glass-bottom boats designed
for tours of the reef. The *Wolf* (tel. 305/296–9653) is a
schooner that sails on day cruises with live music and bills
itself as the "Flagship of the Conch Republic." The *Linda
D III* and *Linda D IV* (tel. 305/296–9798 or 800/299–9798),
captained by third-generation Key West seaman Bill Wick-
ers, run sportfishing outings. The Chamber of Commerce
on Wall Street has a list of other operators.

GOLF

Key West Golf Club (tel. 305/294–5232) is an 18-hole
course on the bay side of Stock Island. Passengers are
charged $95 November to May and $65 June to October.

WATER SPORTS

The northernmost living coral reef in the Americas and clear,
warm Gulf of Mexico waters make Key West a good choice
for getting your flippers wet (*see* Shore Excursions, *above*,
and Beaches, *below*). The excursions of **Captain's Corner**
(0 Duval St., tel. 305/296–8865) last about four hours and
leave at 9:30 and 1:30 (shallow reef diving and snorkeling)
and at 10 (wreck and outer reef diving).

Beaches

Facing the Gulf of Mexico, **Simonton Street Beach,** at the
north end of Simonton Street and near the cruise-ship piers,
is a great place to watch the boats come and go in the harbor. On the Atlantic Ocean, **Fort Zachary Taylor State Historic Site** has several hundred yards of beach near the
western end of Key West. The beach is relatively uncrowded;
snorkeling is good here. **Smathers Beach** features almost 2
mi (3 km) of coarse sand alongside South Roosevelt Boulevard. Vendors along the road will rent you rafts, Windsurfers,
and other beach toys. **Southernmost Beach** is found at the
foot of Duval Street (*see* Exploring Key West, *above*).

Dining

$$$ **Louie's Backyard.** If you're here on a clear day, there's no better place to be than Louie's—right on the water on a tiered terrace lit with tiny white lights in the evening. Come early for a drink at a table so close to the water you could lean over the rail and pick up some driftwood. The menu changes seasonally, but always features creative mixes of Continental cuisine with flavors of the Caribbean and South Florida. The lunch menu is significantly less expensive. *700 Waddell Ave., tel. 305/294–1061. AE, DC, MC, V.*

$–$$ **Rick's Blue Heaven.** Hemingway refereed boxing matches at this renovated clapboard Greek Revival house, once a bordello. Delicious natural foods and West Indian cuisine are served downstairs in the dining room and in the big, leafy yard. Three meals are served six days a week; Sunday there's a to-die-for brunch. Expect a line. *729 Thomas St., tel. 305/296–8666. Reservations not accepted. D, MC, V.*

Pub Crawling

Three spots stand out for first-timers among the many local saloons frequented by Key West denizens. **Capt. Tony's Saloon** (428 Greene St.) is where Ernest Hemingway used to hang out when it was called **Sloppy Joe's.** Nearby, **Sloppy Joe's** (201 Duval St.) has become a landmark in its own right. **Schooner Wharf** (Historic Seaport at Key West Bight, *see* Exploring Key West, *above*) is the most authentically local saloon, and it doesn't sell T-shirts. All are within easy walking distance of the cruise-ship piers.

Martinique

One of the most beautiful islands in the Caribbean, Martinique is lush with wild orchids, frangipani, anthurium, jade vines, flamingo flowers, and hundreds of hibiscus varieties. Trees bend under the weight of tropical treats such as mangoes, papayas, lemons, limes, and bright red West Indian cherries. Acres of banana plantations, pineapple fields, and waving sugarcane stretch to the horizon.

The towering mountains and verdant rain forest in the north lure hikers, while underwater sights and sunken treasures attract snorkelers and scuba divers. Martinique is also wonderful if your idea of exercise is turning over every 10 or 15 minutes to get an even tan, or if your adventuresome spirit is satisfied by a duty-free shop.

The largest of the Windward Islands, Martinique is 6,817 km (4,261 mi) from Paris, but its spirit and language are decidedly French, with more than a soupçon of West Indian spice. Tangible, edible evidence of the fact is the island's cuisine, a superb blend of French and Creole dishes.

Fort-de-France is the capital, but at the turn of the 20th century, St-Pierre, farther up the coast, was Martinique's premier city. Then, in 1902, volcanic Mont Pelée blanketed the city in ash, killing all its residents save for a condemned man in prison. Today, the ruins are a popular excursion for cruise passengers.

Currency

Legal tender is the French franc, which consists of 100 centimes. At press time, the rate was 5.65F to US$1. Dollars are accepted, but it's better to convert a small amount of money into francs. There's an ATM at the Banque Nationale de Paris (BNP) at the northern end of La Savane in Fort-de-France. All prices given below are in U.S. dollars unless otherwise indicated.

Telephones

You can't make collect calls from Martinique to the United States on the local phone system, but you can use a calling card. There are no coin phone booths. Public telephones now use a télécarte; you can buy these at post offices, *café-tabacs* (café-tobacco stores), and *bureaux de change* (currency-exchange offices). Long-distance calls made with télécartes are less costly than operator-assisted calls.

Shore Excursions

The following is a good choice on Martinique. It may not be offered by all cruise lines. Times and prices are approximate.

ISLAND SIGHTS

Martinique's Pompeii. By bus or taxi, drive through the lush green mountains, past picturesque villages, to St-Pierre, stopping at the museum there. This is one of the best island tours in the Caribbean. *4 hrs. Cost: $54.*

Coming Ashore

Cruise ships that dock call at the Maritime Terminal east of the city. The only practical way to get into town is by cab ($16 round-trip). To reach the Maritime Terminal tourist information office, turn right and walk along the waterfront. Ships that anchor in the Baie des Flamands (*see* Exploring Martinique, *below*) tender passengers directly to the downtown waterfront. A tourist office is just across the street from the landing pier in the Air France building. Guided walking tours ($15 for 1½ hrs) can be arranged at the nearby open-air marketplace.

Before hiring a taxi driver, especially for an island tour, make sure his English (or your French) is up to par. Taxis are expensive. The minimum charge is 10F (about $2.90), but a journey of any distance can easily cost upwards of 50F. To get to the beaches and restaurants at Trois Islets will cost you well over 200F. A 40% surcharge is in effect between 8 PM and 6 AM and on Sunday. For a radio cab call 596/63–63–62 or 596/63–10–10.

Exploring Martinique

Numbers in the margin correspond to points of interest on the Martinique map.

FORT-DE-FRANCE

1 The capital city of **Fort-de-France** lies on the island's west coast. With its historic fort and superb setting beneath the towering Pitons du Carbet on the Baie des Flamands, Martinique's capital should be a grand place. It isn't. The most pleasant districts, such as Bellevue and Schoelcher, are on the hillside, and you need a car to reach them. But if you do drive, you may find yourself trapped in gridlock in the warren of narrow streets that is the center of town. True, there are some good shops with Parisian wares (at Parisian prices) and lively street markets that sell, among other things, human hair for wigs. But the heat, exhaust fumes, and litter tend to make exploring here a chore.

Bordering the waterfront is **La Savane,** a rather sad 12½-acre landscaped park filled with rundown gardens, tropical trees, and broken fountains. It's a popular gathering place, though, and is the setting for promenades, parades, and im-

118

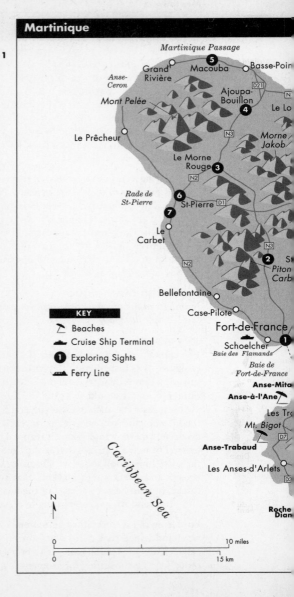

Martinique

Martinique Passage

Grand
Rivière

Macouba **5**

Basse-Poin

*Anse-
Ceron*

Ajoupa-
Bouillon **4**

Le Lo

Mont Pelée

Morne
Jakob

Le Prêcheur

Le Morne
Rouge **3**

*Rade de
St-Pierre*

St-Pierre **6**

7

Le
Carbet

2 St
Piton
Carb

Bellefontaine

KEY

≥ Beaches

⛴ Cruise Ship Terminal

1 Exploring Sights

⛴ Ferry Line

Case-Pilote

Fort-de-France **1**

Schoelcher
Baie des Flamands

*Baie de
Fort-de-France*

Anse-Mita

Anse-à-l'Ane ≥

Les Tro

Mt. Bigot

Anse-Trabaud

Les Anses-d'Arlets ≥

Caribbean Sea

N

Roche
Dian

0 ———————— 10 miles

0 ———————— 15 km

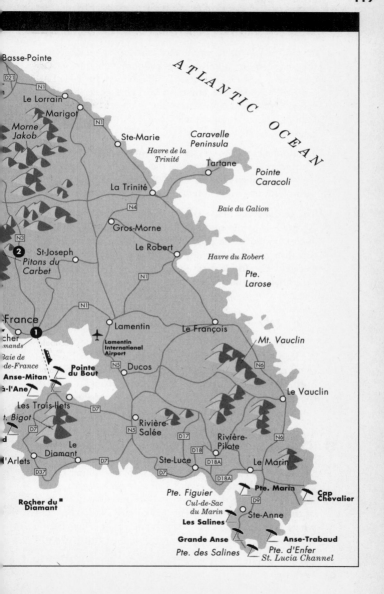

Basse-Pointe
D21
N1
Le Lorrain
Marigot
Morne Jakob
Ste-Marie
N1
Havre de la Trinité
Caravelle Peninsula
Tartane
Pointe Caracoli
La Trinité
N4
Baie du Galion
Gros-Morne
N3
Le Robert
2 St-Joseph
Pitons du Carbet
Havre du Robert
Pte. Larose
N1
France
1
cher mands
Lamentin
Le François
Mt. Vauclin
Lamentin International Airport
Baie de de-France
Anse-Mitan
à-l'Ane
Pointe du Bout
N5
Ducos
N6
Les Trois-Îlets
D7
Le Vauclin
t. Bigot
D7
Le Diamant
Rivière-Salée
N5
D17
Rivière-Pilote
D18
d
l'Arlets
D7
Ste-Luce
D18A
Le Marin
N6
D37
D7
D18A
Pte. Marin
Cpp Chevalier
Rocher du Diamant
Pte. Figuier
D9
Cul-de-Sac du Marin
Les Salines
Ste-Anne
Grande Anse
Anse-Trabaud
Pte. des Salines
Pte. d'Enfer
St. Lucia Channel

ATLANTIC OCEAN

promptu soccer matches. Near the harbor is a marketplace where beads, baskets, pottery, and straw hats are sold.

Rue Victor Schoelcher (pronounced shell-*share*) runs through the center of the capital's primary shopping district—a six-block area bounded by rue de la République, rue de la Liberté, rue Victor Sévère, and rue Victor Hugo (*see* Shopping, *below*). Schoelcher, for whom the road is named, led the fight to free the slaves in the French West Indies in the 19th century.

The Romanesque **St-Louis Cathedral** (west of rue Schoelcher), whose steeple rises high above the surrounding buildings, has lovely stained-glass windows. A number of Martinique's former governors are interred beneath the choir loft.

The **Bibliothèque Schoelcher,** a wildly elaborate Byzantine-Egyptian-Romanesque public library, was built in 1887 and exhibited at the 1889 Paris Exposition, after which it was dismantled, shipped to Martinique, and reassembled piece by piece. Inside the eye-popping structure is a collection of ancient documents recounting Fort-de-France's development. *Corner of rue de la Liberté and rue Perrinon, tel. 596/70–26–67. Admission free. Open Mon. 1–5:30, Tues.–Thurs. 8:30–6, Fri. 8:30–noon.*

THE NORTH

A nice way to see the lush island interior and St-Pierre is to take the N3, which snakes through dense rain forests, north through the mountains to Le Morne Rouge, then take the coastal N2 back to Fort-de-France via St-Pierre. You can do the 64-km (40-mi) round-trip in an afternoon.

The first stop along the N3 (also called the Route de la Trace) ❷ is **Balata** to see the Balata Church, an exact replica of Sacré-Coeur Basilica in Paris, and the *Jardin de Balata* (Balata Gardens; tel. 596/64–48–73). Jean-Phillipe Thoze, a professional landscaper and devoted horticulturist, spent 20 years creating this collection of thousands of varieties of tropical flowers and plants. There are shaded benches where you can take in the panoramic views. The gardens are open daily from 9 to 5; admission is 35 francs.

On the southern slopes of Mont Pelée along the N3 is ❸ **Le Morne Rouge.** Like St-Pierre, this town was destroyed by the volcano in 1902 and is now a popular resort. Signs will direct you to the narrow road that takes you halfway up the mountain—you won't really have time to hike to the 4,600-ft peak, but this side trip gets you fairly close and offers spectacular views.

④ A few kilometers south of Basse-Pointe, heading northeast on the N3 toward the Atlantic coast, is the flower-filled village of **Ajoupa-Bouillon.** This 17th-century settlement in the midst of pineapple fields is beautiful, but skip it if you've never seen St-Pierre and are running out of time. From Le Morne Rouge, you'll need a good three hours to enjoy the coastal drive back to Fort-de-France.

⑤ If you opt to explore the northeast coast, head for **Macouba.** Its cliff-top location affords magnificent views of the sea, the mountains, and—on clear days—the neighboring island of Dominica. JM Distillery produces the best *rhum vieux* (aged rum) on the island. A tour and samples are free. *JM Distillery, on main road, Macouba, tel. 596/78–92–55. Admission free. Open weekdays 7–noon and 1:30–3:30.*

Macouba is also the starting point for another spectacular drive, the 10-km (6-mi) route to Grand-Rivière on the northernmost point. This is Martinique at its greenest. Groves of giant bamboo, curtains of vines hanging over cliffs, and 7-ft-high tree ferns seem to grow as you watch them. At the end of the road is Grand-Rivière, a fishing village at the foot of high cliffs and, literally, the end of the road.

⑥ **St-Pierre** (southwest of Le Morne Rouge on the N2) is the island's oldest city. It was once called the Paris of the West Indies, but Mont Pelée changed all that in the spring of 1902, when the mountain began to rumble and spit steam. By the first week in May, all wildlife had wisely vacated the area, but city officials ignored the warnings, needing voters in town for an upcoming election. On the morning of May 8, the volcano erupted, belching forth a cloud of burning ash with temperatures above 3,600°F. Within three minutes, Mont Pelée had transformed St-Pierre into Martinique's Pompeii. The entire town was annihilated, its 30,000 inhabitants calcified. There was only one survivor: a prisoner named Cyparis, who was saved by the thick walls of his underground cell. He was later pardoned and became a sideshow attraction at the Barnum & Bailey Circus.

You can wander through the site to see the ruins of the island's first church, built in 1640; the theater; the toppled statues; and Cyparis's cell. The *Cyparis Express* is a small tourist train that runs through the city, hitting the important sights with a running narrative (in French). *Train departs from pl. des Ruines du Figuier, tel. 596/55–50–92. Tickets: 30F. Runs every 45 min, weekdays 9:30–1 and 2:30–5:30; call for exact times.*

While in St-Pierre, which now has only 6,000 residents, you might pick up some delicious French pastries to nibble on your return trip after a visit to the **Musée Vulcanologique.** Established in 1932 by American volcanologist Franck Perret, the collection includes photographs of the old town, documents, and excavated relics, including molten glass, melted iron, and contorted clocks stopped at 8 AM, the time of the eruption. *Rue Victor Hugo, tel. 596/78–15–16. Admission: 15F. Open daily 9–noon and 3–5.*

A short way south of St-Pierre is Anse Turin, where Paul Gauguin lived briefly in 1887 with his friend and fellow ❼ artist Charles Laval. The **Musée Gauguin** traces the history of the artist's Martinique connection through documents, letters, and reproductions of paintings. *Tel. 596/77–22–66. Admission: 15F. Open daily 9–5:30.*

Shopping

French products, such as perfume, wines, liquors, designer scarves, leather goods, and crystal, are all good buys in Fort-de-France. In addition, luxury goods are discounted 20% when paid for with traveler's checks or major credit cards. Look for Creole gold jewelry; white and dark rums; and handcrafted straw goods, pottery, and tapestries.

Small shops that sell luxury items are abundant around the cathedral in Fort-de-France, particularly on rue Victor Hugo, rue Moreau de Jones, rue Antoine Siger, and rue Lamartine. Look for Lalique, Limoges, and Baccarat at **Cadet Daniel** (72 rue Antoine Siger, tel. 596/71–41–48) and at **Roger Albert** (7 rue Victor Hugo, tel. 596/71–71–71), which also sells perfume. A wide variety of authentic local crafts is available at the **Centre des Métiers d'Art** (Rue Ernest Deproge,

The first thing you need overseas is the one thing you forget to pack.

FOREIGN CURRENCY DELIVERED OVERNIGHT

Chase Currency To Go® delivers foreign currency to your home by the next business day*

It's easy–before you travel, call 1-888-CHASE84 for delivery of any of 75 currencies

Delivery is free with orders of $500 or more

Competitive rates– without exchange fees

You don't have to be a Chase customer–you can pay by Visa® or MasterCard®

 CHASE

THE RIGHT RELATIONSHIP IS EVERYTHING®

1•888•CHASE84
www.chase.com

Distinctive guides packed with up-to-date expert
advice and smart choices for every type of traveler.

Fodor's. For the world of ways you travel.

tel. 596/70–25–01). The **Galerie Arti-Bijoux** (89 rue Victor
Hugo, tel. 596/63–10–62) has some unusual and excellent
Haitian art at reasonable prices.

Sports

FISHING

For charter excursions, contact **Bathy's Club** (Hôtel Méridien, Anse-Mitan, tel. 596/66–00–00).

GOLF

Golf Country Club de la Martinique (tel. 596/68–32–81) has
an 18-hole Robert Trent Jones–designed course with an English-speaking pro, a pro shop, a bar, and a restaurant. At
Trois-Ilets, 1½ km (1 mi) from the Pointe du Bout resort
area and 29 km (18 mi) from Fort-de-France, the club offers special greens fees for cruise-ship passengers.

HIKING

Parc Naturel Régional de la Martinique (9 bd. Général de
Gaulle, Fort-de-France, tel. 596/73–19–30) organizes inexpensive guided hiking tours. Information is available at
the island tourist offices.

HORSEBACK RIDING

Excursions and lessons are available at the **Black Horse Ranch**
(near La Pagerie, Trois-Ilets, tel. 596/68–37–80), **La Cav-
ale** (Pointe de la Chery, Le Diamant, tel. 596/76–22–94),
and **Ranch Jack** (near Anse-d'Arlets, tel. 596/68–37–69).

WATER SPORTS

At hotel beach shacks, you can rent Hobie Cats, Sunfish,
and Sailfish by the hour. If you're a member of a yacht club,
show your club membership card and enjoy the facilities
of **Club de la Voile de Fort-de-France** (Pointe Simon, tel. 596/
70–26–63) and **Yacht Club de la Martinique** (blvd. Chevalier, Ste-Marthe, tel. 596/63–26–76). To explore the old shipwrecks, coral gardens, and other undersea sites, you must
have a medical certificate and insurance papers. Among the
island's dive operators are **Bathy's Club** (Hotel Méridien,
Anse-Mitan, tel. 596/66–00–00) and the **Okeanos Club**
(Le Diamant, tel. 596/76–21–76).

Beaches

Topless bathing is prevalent at the large resort hotels. Unless you're an expert swimmer, steer clear of the Atlantic

waters, except in the area of Cap Chevalier and the Caravelle Peninsula. **Anse-à-l'Ane** offers picnic tables and a nearby shell museum; bathers cool off in the bar of Le Calalou Hotel. **Anse-Mitan** is a white-sand beach with superb snorkeling. **Pointe du Bout** has small, white-sand beaches, most of which are commandeered by resort hotels. **Les Salines** is the best of Martinique's beaches, whether you choose to be with other sun worshipers or to find your own quiet stretch of sand. However, it's at least an hour's drive from Fort-de-France and 8 km (5 mi) beyond Ste-Anne.

Dining

All restaurants include a 15% service charge in their prices.

$$ **Le Fromager.** If you're touring the north of the island, don't miss this beautiful restaurant perched high above St-Pierre, with smashing views of the town's red roofs and the sea beyond. Superlative choices include crayfish colombo, marinated octopus, and duck fillet. *On the road to Fond St-Denis, tel. 596/78– 19–07. AE, DC, MC, V.*

$$ **Le Ruisseau Restaurant at Leyritz Plantation.** Upon disembarking, negotiate a good price from a cab driver and treat yourself to a ride to lunch at this lovely restaurant in the northern portion of Martinique. It's an exhilarating trip full of hairpin curves and wonderful views of the island. At Le Ruisseau, you'll find roasted conch in the shell, fresh salads, red snapper, grilled lamb and assorted fruit. Stroll the gorgeous grounds before starting back. *Basse-Pointe, tel. 596/78–53–92. Reservations essential. MC, V.*

$ **Le Marie Sainte.** Looking for a great lunch? Search no farther than a couple of blocks from your boat. Prix-fixe lunches start at 75F. Try the succulent *daube de poisson* (braised fish) or any specials of the day. *160 rue Victor Hugo, tel. 56/70–00–30, AE, MC, V. Closed Sun. No dinner.*

Nassau, the Bahamas

The 17th-century town of Nassau, the capital of the Bahamas, has witnessed Spanish invasions and hosted pirates, who made it their headquarters for raids along the Spanish Main. The new American navy seized Ft. Montagu here in 1776, when they won a victory without firing a shot.

The heritage of old Nassau blends the Southern charm of British loyalists from the Carolinas, the African tribal traditions of freed slaves, and a bawdy history of blockade-running during the Civil War and rum-running in the Roaring Twenties. Over it all is a subtle layer of civility and sophistication, derived from three centuries of British rule.

Reminders of the island's British heritage are everywhere in Nassau. Court justices sport wigs and scarlet robes. The police wear colonial garb: starched white jackets, red-striped navy trousers, and tropical pith helmets. Traffic keeps to the left, and the language has a British-colonial lilt, softened by a slight drawl. Nassau's charm, however, is often lost in its commercialism. There's excellent shopping, but if you look past the duty-free shops, you'll also find some sights of historical significance that are worth seeing.

Shore Excursions
The following are good choices in Nassau. Times and prices are approximate.

UNDERSEA CREATURES
Crystal Cay (tel. 242/328–1036). This excursion provides convenient transportation by ferry, where a 100-ft observation tower soars above the landscape, but the real views are of turtles, stingrays, and starfish below the water. The ferry leaves the cruise-ship docks at regular intervals. *Cost: $2 per trip; admission to Crystal Cay, $16.*

Dolphin Encounters (tel. 242/363–1653 or 242/363–1003). Close Encounter excursions ($49 per person) are offered on Blue Lagoon Island (Salt Cay), just east of Paradise Island. Sit on a platform with your feet in the water while dolphins play around you, or wade in the waist-deep water to get up close and personal with them. Trainers are available to answer questions. Swim-with-the-Dolphins ($115 per person) allows you to actually swim with these friendly creatures for about 30 minutes. Programs are very popular, so make reservations as early as possible. Programs are available daily, 8–5:30.

Coming Ashore
Cruise ships dock at one of three piers on Prince George's Wharf. Taxi drivers who meet the ships may offer you a

$2 ride into town, but the historic government buildings and duty-free shops lie just steps from the dock area. As you leave the pier, look for a tall pink tower: diagonally across from here is the tourist information office. Stop in for maps of the island and downtown Nassau. On most days you can join a 45-minute walking tour ($2 per person) conducted by well-trained guides. Tours generally start every hour on the hour 11 AM–4 PM, but stop in or call to confirm. Outside the office, an ATM dispenses U.S. dollars.

As you disembark from your ship you will find a row of taxis and air-conditioned limousines. The latter are Nassau's fleet of tour cars. Taxi fares are fixed at $2.50 for the first ½ km (¼ mi), 30¢ each additional ½ km (¼ mi). Sightseeing tours cost about $50 per hour.

Also along the wharf are surreys drawn by straw-hatted horses that will take you through the old city. The cost is $10 per person for two or more for 25 minutes, but verify prices before getting on.

For the more adventurous, scooters may be rented as you exit Prince George's Wharf. Rates average $40 per half day, $50 per full day. Helmets are mandatory and provided.

To get to Paradise Island, take the ferry from the dock area ($4 each way).

Currency

The Bahamian dollar is the official currency of the Bahamas. Since the U.S. dollar is universally accepted, however, there's really no need to change any money to Bahamian currency. Prices quoted throughout this chapter are in U.S. dollars unless otherwise indicated.

Telephones

Calling locally or internationally is easy in the Bahamas. To place a local call, dial the seven-digit phone number. To call the United States, dial 1 plus the area code. Pay phones cost 25¢ per call; Bahamian and U.S. quarters are accepted, as are BATELCO phone cards. To place a call using your own calling card, use your long-distance carrier's access code or dial 0 for the operator, who will then place the call using your card number.

Exploring Nassau

Numbers in the margin correspond to points of interest on the Nassau map.

❶ As you leave the cruise wharf, you can't miss **Parliament Square.** Dating from the early 1800s and patterned after southern U.S. Colonial architecture, this cluster of pink, colonnaded buildings with green shutters is striking. In the center of the square is a statue of the young Queen Victoria.

❷ For a great view (and a real workout), climb the **Queen's Staircase,** a famous Nassau landmark found at the head of Elizabeth Avenue. Its 65 steps, thought to have been hewn from the coral limestone cliff by slaves in the late 18th century, were designed to provide a direct route between town and Ft. Fincastle. The staircase was named more than a hundred years later, in honor of Queen Victoria's reign.

❸ **Ft. Fincastle** is easily recognized by its shape—it resembles the bow of a ship. Built in 1793, it never fired a shot in battle but served as a lookout and signal tower.

For a really spectacular view of the island of New Providence, climb the 225 steps (or ride the elevator) to the top
❹ of the **Water Tower.** Rising to 126 ft, more than 200 ft above sea level, the tower is the highest point on the island.

❺ The most interesting fort on the island is **Ft. Charlotte,** built in 1787 replete with a waterless moat, a drawbridge, ramparts, and dungeons. Like Ft. Fincastle, no shots were ever fired from this fort. Ft. Charlotte is at the top of a hill and commands a fine view of Nassau Harbor and Arawak Cay, a small, man-made island that is home to the fish fry where you can pick up a delicious, inexpensive lunch. *Off W. Bay St. at Chippingham Rd., tel. 242/322–7500. Admission free. Local guides conduct tours Mon.–Sat. 8:30–4.*

❻ The **Ardastra Gardens and Zoo,** 5 acres of tropical greenery and flowering shrubs, contain exotic animals from around the world and an aviary of rare tropical birds. The gardens are renowned for the pink, spindly legged, marching flamingos that perform daily at 11, 2, and 4. The flamingo, by the way, is the national bird of the Bahamas. *Near Ft. Charlotte, off Chippingham Rd., tel. 242/323–5806. Admission: $12. Open daily 9–5.*

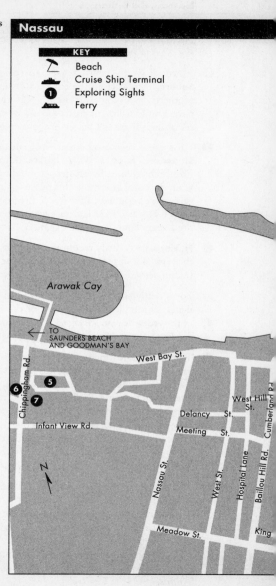

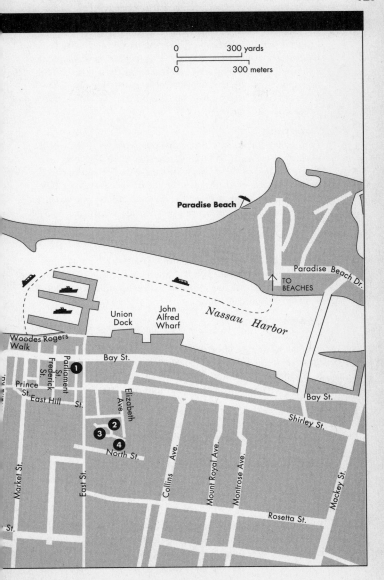

Across the street from the Ardastra Gardens and Zoo are
⑦ the **Nassau Botanic Gardens.** On the gardens' 18-acre
grounds are 600 species of flowering trees and shrubs; two
freshwater ponds with lilies, water plants, and tropical
fish; and a small cactus garden that ends in a grotto. The
many trails are perfect for leisurely strolls. *Near Ft. Charlotte, off Chippingham Rd., tel. 242/323–5975. Admission:
$1. Open weekdays 9–5.*

Shopping
Forbes magazine once claimed that the two cities in the world
with the best buys on wristwatches were Hong Kong and
Nassau. Most of the stores selling these and other duty-free
items are clustered along an eight-block stretch of Bay
Street in Old Nassau or spill over onto a few side streets
downtown. Most stores are open Monday–Saturday 9–5.
The straw market is open seven days a week. Most shops
accept major credit cards.

If you're interested in old-fashioned maps and prints, seek
out **Balmain Antiques** (308 Bay St., tel. 242/323–7421). It's
a little hard to find: the doorway to the second-floor gallery
is on the side of the building.

Sports
FISHING
Contact **Chubasco Charters** (tel. 242/322–8148) or **Brown's
Charters** (tel. 242/324–1215). Boat charters cost from $350
to $600 for a half day, depending on the size of the boat.
Full-day charters are double the half-day rate.

GOLF
Three excellent 18-hole courses are open to the public:
Cable Beach Golf Course (opposite the Superclubs Breezes,
tel. 242/327–6000; 800/222–7466 in the U. S.), **Paradise
Island Golf Club** (eastern end of Paradise Island, tel. 242/
363–3925; 800/321–3000 in the U. S.), and **South Ocean
Golf Club** (tel. 242/362–4391). Fees are $45–$155.

PARASAILING
Parasailing is available from **Sea & Ocean Sports** at the Sher-
aton Grand Resort on Paradise Island (tel. 242/363–3500,
ext. 6142). A six-minute ride costs $40.

Beaches

Paradise Beach stretches for more than 1½ km (1 mi) on the western end of Paradise Island. On the north side of the island lies **Cabbage Beach,** which is popular with locals and tourists alike and the home of most of the island's resorts. The **Western Esplanade** sweeps westward from the British Colonial Hotel on Bay Street (a 10-min walk from the cruise-ship pier). It's just across the street from shops and restaurants, and it has rest rooms, a snack bar, and changing facilities. A little farther west is **Saunders Beach. Goodman's Bay,** a bit farther west of Saunders, is popular with Bahamians for picnics and cookouts.

Dining

$$$ **Graycliff.** Situated in a magnificent, 200-year-old colonial mansion, Graycliff is filled with antiques and English country-house charm. The outstanding Continental and Bahamian menu includes beluga caviar, grouper in cream and Dijon mustard, and chateaubriand, with elegant pastries and flaming coffees for dessert. The wine cellar is excellent. Graycliff offers its own hand-rolled cigars of Cuban tobacco— made on the premises. *W. Hill St., across from Government House, tel. 242/322–2796 or 800/633–7411. Reservations essential. Jacket required. AE, D, DC, MC, V.*

$$ **Native's.** For a purely Bahamian experience, try this winning spot in an old Nassau house, with a shady yard for outdoor dining. Local favorites like cracked conch and fried snapper are served with mounds of peas 'n' rice, the typical Bahamian side dish. *E. Bay St. at Maud St., tel. 242/394–8280. Closed Mon. AE, D, MC, V.*

$$ **Poop Deck.** A nautical air fills this favorite haunt of Nassau residents. Tables overlook the harbor and Paradise Island. Cuisine is exceptional Bahamian-style seafood, served in a festive, friendly atmosphere. Save room for guava duff, a warm guava-layered local dessert, and a Calypso coffee, spiked with secret ingredients. *E. Bay St. (an 8-min cab ride from the pier), tel. 242/393–8175. AE, DC, MC, V.*

$ **Crocodiles Waterfront Bar & Restaurant.** Watching the cruise ships come and go (hopefully, not your own) is just one of the attractions of this relaxing harborside restaurant. The tropical setting (thatched tiki huts) makes it fun for all ages. Bahamian dishes and burgers are the specialties of the house. *E. Bay St., tel. 242/323–3341. Reservations not accepted. D, MC, V.*

Nightlife

Some ships stay late into the night or until the next day so that passengers can enjoy Nassau's nightlife. You'll find non-stop entertainment nightly along Cable Beach and on Paradise Island. All the larger hotels offer lounges with island combos for listening or dancing, and restaurants with soft guitar or piano background music.

CASINOS

The two casinos—**Crystal Palace Casino on Cable Beach** and **Paradise Island Resort and Casino**—open early in the day and remain active into the wee hours of the morning. Visitors must be 18 or older to enter a casino, 21 or older to gamble.

NIGHTCLUBS

Club Waterloo (E. Bay St., tel. 242/393–7324) is one of Nassau's most swinging nightspots. Music can be heard nightly at **The Zoo** (Saunders Beach, tel. 242/322–7195)

LOCAL ENTERTAINMENT

King & Knights (tel. 242/327–5321), at the Nassau Beach Hotel showroom, is a native show featuring world-famous King Eric and his Knights. The show is the only one of its kind on the island with steel drums, unbelievable limbo feats, fire dancing, Bahamian music, song, and dance. Dinner is at 7, followed by two shows at 8:30 and 10:30, Tuesday through Saturday. One show is held Sunday and Monday at 8:30.

Panama Canal

Transit of the Panama Canal takes only one day. The rest of your cruise will be spent on islands in the Caribbean or at ports along the Mexican Riviera. Increasingly, Panama Canal itineraries include stops in Central America; some may also call along the northern coast of South America. Most Panama Canal cruises are one-way trips, part of a 10- to 14-day cruise between the Atlantic and Pacific oceans. Shorter loop cruises enter the canal from the Caribbean, sail around Gatún Lake for a few hours, and return to the Caribbean.

The Panama Canal is best described as a water bridge that raises ships up and over Central America, then lets them down again, using a series of locks or water steps. Artificially created Gatún Lake, 85 ft above sea level, is the canal's highest point. The route is approximately 80 km (50 mi) long, and the crossing takes from eight to 10 hours. Cruise ships pay more than $100,000 for each transit, which is less than half of what it would cost them to sail around Cape Horn, at the southern tip of South America.

Just before dawn, your ship will line up with dozens of other vessels to await its turn to enter the canal. Before it can proceed, two pilots and a narrator will come on board. The sight of a massive cruise ship being raised dozens of feet into the air by water is so fascinating that passengers will crowd all the forward decks at the first lock. If you can't see, go to the rear decks, where there is usually more room and the view is just as intriguing. Later in the day you won't find as many passengers up front.

On and off throughout the day, commentary is broadcast over the ship's loudspeakers, imparting facts and figures as well as anecdotes about the history of the canal. The canal stands where it does today not because it's the best route but because the railroad was built there first, making access to the area relatively easy. The railway had followed an old Spanish mule trail that had been there for more than 300 years.

St. Croix

St. Croix is the largest of the three U.S. Virgin Islands (USVI) that form the northern hook of the Lesser Antilles, and it's 64 km (40 mi) south of its sister islands, St. Thomas and St. John. Christopher Columbus landed here in 1493, skirmishing briefly with the native Carib Indians. Since then, the USVI have played a colorful, if painful, role as pawns in the game of European colonialism. Theirs is a history of pirates and privateers, sugar plantations, slave trading, and slave revolt and liberation. Through it all, Denmark had staying power. From the 17th to the 19th century, Danes oversaw a plantation slave economy that produced molasses, rum, cotton, and tobacco. Many of the stones you tread on in the streets were once used as ballast on sailing ships, and the yellow fort of Christiansted is a reminder of the value once placed on this island treasure.

Currency

The U.S. dollar is the official currency of St. Croix.

Telephones

Calling the United States from St. Croix is just like calling in the United States. Local calls from a public phone cost 25¢ for every five minutes.

Shore Excursions

The following are good choices on St. Croix. They may not be offered by all cruise lines. Times and prices are approximate.

ISLAND SIGHTS

Bicycle Jaunt. Ride along St. Croix's coast and through Frederiksted before heading along Northside Road. The 19-km (12-mi) trip will take you past ruins, historical sights, tropical forests, rolling hills, and ocean views. Bicycles and equipment are included. *3 hrs. Cost: $35.*

TEE TIME

Golf at Carambola. Robert Trent Jones designed this 18-hole, par-72 course, considered one of the Caribbean's finest. *Half day. Cost: $70–$100.*

Coming Ashore

Larger cruise ships dock in Frederiksted; smaller ships dock at Gallows Bay, outside Christiansted. You'll find information centers at both piers, and both towns are easy to explore on foot. Beaches are nearby.

Taxis of all shapes and sizes are available at the cruise-ship piers and at various shopping and resort areas. Remember, too, that you can hail a taxi that's already occupied. Drivers take multiple fares and sometimes even trade passengers at midpoints. Taxis don't have meters, so you should check the list of official rates (available at the visitor centers or from drivers) and agree on a fare before you start. Try the **St. Croix Taxi Association** (tel. 340/778–1088) or **Antilles Taxi Service** (tel. 340/773–5020).

Exploring St. Croix

Numbers in the margin correspond to points of interest on the St. Croix map.

① **Frederiksted** speaks to history buffs with its quaint Victorian architecture and historic fort. There's very little traffic, so this is the perfect place for strolling and shopping.

Ft. Frederik, completed in the late 18th century, sits adjacent to the cruise-ship pier. Here, in 1848, 8,000 slaves marched on the redbrick fort to demand their freedom. Governor Peter van Scholten, fearing they would burn the town to the ground, granted it.

Within walking distance of the pier are **St. Paul's Anglican Church,** built in 1812, and **St. Patrick's Catholic Church,** built in 1843 of coral. Walk 3 blocks inland to reach Prince Street. St. Patrick's is to the east, St. Paul's to the west.

② The **Karl and Marie Lawaetz Museum,** on a circa 1750 farm, takes you on a trip back to the time when Denmark owned St. Croix. A Lawaetz family member shows you the four-poster bed where Karl and Marie slept and the china Marie painted herself. The taxi fare from Frederiksted for two people is $6. From Christiansted, the fare is $21. *Estate Little LaGrange, tel. 340/772–1539. Admission: $5. Open Tues.–Sat. 10–4.*

③ **West End Salt Pond** is rife with mangroves and little blue herons. In the spring, large leatherback sea turtles clamber up the white sand across the road to lay their eggs. You will also see brown pelicans. Because the location is remote, for safety's sake it's better to ask your taxi driver to include it on a tour rather go on your own.

With its windmill, cookhouse, and other outbuildings, the **④** lovingly restored **Estate Whim Plantation Museum** gives a real sense of what life was like for the owners of St. Croix's sugar plantations in the 1800s. The great house, with a singular oval shape and high ceilings, features antique furniture and utensils, as well as a major apothecary exhibit. Note the house's fresh, airy atmosphere—the waterless moat was used not for defense but for gathering cooling air. A taxi trip for two from the Frederiksted pier will run $4. From

136

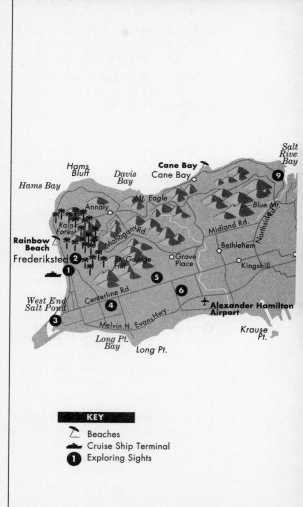

St. Croix

KEY

Beaches
Cruise Ship Terminal
Exploring Sights

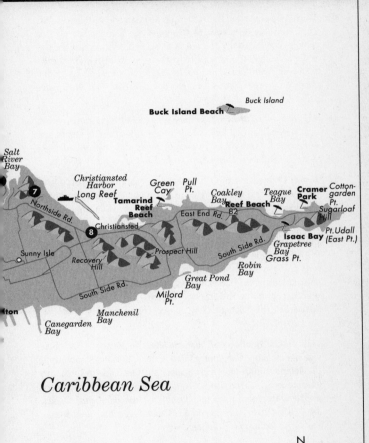

Buck Island

Buck Island Beach

*Salt
River
Bay*

*Christiansted
Harbor*
Long Reef

*Green
Cay*

*Pull
Pt.*

*Coakley
Bay*

*Teague
Bay*

**Cramer
Park**

*Cotton-
garden
Pt.*

(7)

Northside Rd.

**Tamarind
Reef
Beach**

Reef Beach

*Sugarloaf
Hill*

82

East End Rd.

Christiansted

(8)

South Side Rd.

*Pt.Udall
(East Pt.)*

Isaac Bay

*Grapetree
Bay*

Prospect Hill

Grass Pt.

Sunny Isle

*Recovery
Hill*

*Robin
Bay*

South Side Rd.

*Great Pond
Bay*

*Milord
Pt.*

lton

*Manchenil
Bay*

*Canegarden
Bay*

Caribbean Sea

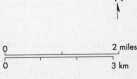

N

0		2 miles
0		3 km

Christiansted, the cost is $20.50. *Rte. 70, tel. 340/772–0598. Admission: $6. Open Mon.–Sat. 10–4.*

⑤ With 17 acres of lush and fragrant flora to explore, the **St. George Village Botanical Gardens** are a must for nature lovers. They occupy the ruins of a 19th-century sugarcane plantation village. A taxi trip for two from the Frederiksted pier costs $6.50. From Christiansted, the cost is $15.50. *Turn north off Rte. 70 at sign, tel. 340/692–2874. Admission: $5. Open daily 9–4.*

⑥ The rum from **Cruzan Distillery** is made with pure rainwater, making it (so they say) superior to any other. Visitors are welcome for a tour and a free rum-laced drink. *W. Airport Rd., 340/692–2280. Admission: $4. Open daily 9–4.*

⑦ **Judith's Fancy.** Within this upscale neighborhood you'll find the ruins of an old great house and tower, both remnants of a circa 1750 Danish sugar plantation. It's named after a woman buried on the property. *Rte. 751.*

⑧ Historic **Christiansted** serves as St. Croix's commercial center. Trade here in the 1700s and 1800s was in sugar, rum, and molasses. Today the town is home to law offices, tourist shops, and restaurants, but many of the structures, which run from the harbor up into the gentle hillsides, date from the 18th century. A taxi for two from Frederiksted costs $20.

Within the **Christiansted Historic Site,** the National Park Service oversees operation of several historic buildings, including the Steeple Building, which housed the first Danish Lutheran Church in St. Croix. Stop in at the yellow Ft. Christiansvaern on the waterfront for a stroll back in time. *Hospital St., tel. 340/773–1460. Admission: $2. Open weekdays 8–5, weekends and holidays 9–5.*

⑨ The **Salt River Bay National Historical Park and Ecological Preserve** encompasses a bio-diverse coastal estuary with the largest remaining mangrove forest in the USVI, a submarine canyon, and several endangered species. This is also where Columbus came ashore in 1493. Directly under the spot where your taxi parks is a ceremonial ball court used by the Carib Indians who lived at the site. *Rte. 80.*

Shopping

The selection of duty-free goods on St. Croix is fairly good.
The best shopping is in **Christiansted,** where most stores are
in the historic district near the harbor. King Street, Strand
Street, and the arcades that lead off them comprise the main
shopping district. The longest arcade is Caravelle Arcade,
adjacent to the hotel of the same name. **Gallows Bay,** just
east of Christiansted, has an attractive boutique area that
features unusual island-made silver jewelry and gift items.
In **Frederiksted,** a handful of shops face the cruise-ship
pier. Try **Island Webe** for locally made products. They
carry tasty jams, original art, and interesting double dolls,
with a black face on one side and a white one on the other.

Sports

GOLF

The 18-hole course at the **Buccaneer** (tel. 340/773–2100)
is close to Christiansted. The **Reef Club** (tel. 340/773–
8844), in the northeast, has 9 holes. More spectacular is
the course at the **Sunterra Carambola Beach Course** (tel. 340/
778–5638), designed by Robert Trent Jones, in a valley in
the northwest. Fees range from $35 to $77.

HORSEBACK RIDING

At Sprat Hall, near Frederiksted, **Paul & Jill's Equestrian
Stables** (tel. 340/772–2627) offers rides through the rain
forest.

WATER SPORTS

Dive Experience (tel. 340/773–3307), one of the island's best
dive specialists and a PADI-certified facility, provides a
range of services from introductory dives to certification.
Mile-Mark Charters (tel. 340/773–2628) offers sailing,
snorkeling, and scuba diving. Both are in Christiansted.

Beaches

Buck Island and its reef can be reached only by boat from
Christiansted but are well worth a visit. The beach is beautiful, but its finest treasures are underwater. At **Cane Bay,**
a breezy north-shore beach, the waters are not always gentle but the diving and snorkeling are wondrous, and there
are never many people around. Five kilometers (three miles)
north of Frederiksted you'll find **West End Beach,** where you
can enjoy the sand, snorkel at a small nearby reef, and get

a bite to eat at the bar. **Tamarind Reef Beach** is a small but attractive beach with good snorkeling east of Christiansted. Green Cay and Buck Island seem smack in front of you—an arresting view.

Dining

$$$ **Le St. Tropez.** A ceramic-tile bar and soft lighting add to the Mediterranean atmosphere at this pleasant bistro off Frederiksted's main thoroughfare. You can sit inside or on the patio to feast on French fare, including salads and grilled meats in delicate sauces. The menu changes daily, often taking advantage of fresh local seafood. *67 King St., tel. 340/772–3000. AE, MC, V. Closed Sun.*

$ **Pizza Mare–Cafe Sol.** This popular lunch spot serves pizza and panini along with exotic coffees and luscious desserts. Try the chocolate suicide cake. *1111 Strand St., tel. 340/773–0553. AE, D, MC, V. No dinner Sun.–Wed.*

St. Kitts and Nevis

Mountainous St. Kitts, the first English settlement in the Leeward Islands, crams some stunning scenery into its 65 square mi (168 square km). Vast, brilliant-green fields of sugarcane run to the shore. The fertile, lush island has some fascinating natural and historical attractions: a rain forest, replete with waterfalls, thick vines, and secret trails; a central mountain range, dominated by the 3,792-ft Mt. Liamuiga, whose crater has long been dormant; and Brimstone Hill, known in the 17th century as the Gibraltar of the West Indies.

In 1493, when Columbus spied a cloud-crowned volcanic isle during his second voyage to the New World, he named it Nieves—the Spanish word for "snows"—because it reminded him of the peaks of the Pyrenees. Nevis rises from the water in an almost perfect cone, the tip of its 3,232-ft central mountain hidden by clouds. Even less developed than St. Kitts, Nevis is known for its long beaches with white and black sand, its lush greenery, and its restored sugar plantations that now house charming inns.

St. Kitts and Nevis, along with Anguilla, achieved self-government as an Associated State of Great Britain in 1967. In 1983, St. Kitts and Nevis became an independent nation. English with a strong West Indian lilt is spoken here.

People are friendly but shy; always ask before you take photographs. Also, be sure to wear wraps or shorts over beach attire when you're in public places.

Currency
Legal tender is the Eastern Caribbean (E.C.) dollar. At press time, the rate of exchange was EC$2.70 to US$1. U.S. dollars are accepted practically everywhere, but you'll usually get change in E.C. currency. Prices quoted throughout this chapter are in U.S. dollars unless otherwise noted.

Telephones
To make a local call, dial the seven-digit number. Pay phones are usually found in major town squares and take E.C. coins or phone cards.

Avoid using the widely advertised Skantel, which ostensibly allows you to make credit-card calls; rates are usurious, and they freeze an outrageous amount for up to a week on your credit card until they put through the exact bill.

Shore Excursions
The following are good choices in St. Kitts and Nevis. They may not be offered by all cruise lines. Times and prices are approximate.

ISLAND SIGHTS
Nevis Highlights. Board the ferry at Basseterre for the 45-minute ride to Nevis. You'll visit Charlestown and the Nelson Museum, and pass old plantations on your way to the Nevis Botanical Gardens. *4 hrs. Cost: $100.*

NATURAL BEAUTY
Nevis Rainforest Adventure. Take the ferry from Basseterre to Charlestown, Nevis, and board a bus to Nevis Peak. On a 75-minute hike, you'll experience the diverse flora and fauna of the rain forest. *4 hrs. Cost: $80.*

UNDERSEA CREATURES
Catamaran Sail and Snorkeling Adventure. Take a catamaran to Smittens Bay, accessible only by sea, where you'll view the area's myriad fish and coral. *3½ hrs. Cost: $70.*

Coming Ashore
Cruise ships calling at St. Kitts and Nevis dock at Port Zante in Basseterre, the capital of St. Kitts. When completed,

Port Zante will comprise a welcome center, hotel and casino, shops, and restaurants. The structure sustained serious damage from Hurricane Georges in 1998, however, and it is unclear when construction will be finished.

On both St. Kitts and Nevis the cruise-ship terminal is located downtown, two minutes' walk from sights and shops. Taxis on the islands are unmetered, but fixed rates, in E.C. dollars, are posted at the jetty. A one-way ride from Basseterre, St. Kitts, to Brimstone Hill costs $28 (for one to four passengers), to Romney Manor costs $24, and to Turtle Beach costs $32. A three-hour driving tour of St. Kitts or Nevis will run you about $50. Before setting off in a cab, be sure to clarify whether the rate quoted is in E.C. or U.S. dollars.

VISITING NEVIS

Nevis is a 45-minute ferry ride from Basseterre. You can tour Charlestown, the capital, in a half hour or so, but you'll need three to four hours to explore the entire island. The 150-passenger government-operated ferry M/V *Caribe Queen* makes the 45-minute crossing from Basseterre, St. Kitts, to Charlestown, Nevis, twice daily except Thursday and Sunday. Given the irregularity and infrequency of ferry departures, your best bet for a visit to Nevis is to sign up for a cruise line–run shore excursion.

There are ample rewards if you decide to explore Nevis independently, but whether this is an option for you will depend largely on your ship's schedule. Depending on the day, the ferry leaves Basseterre either at 7 AM, 7:30 AM, 8 AM, or 1 PM (the latter returning at 6:45 PM). Since most cruise ships arrive in port at around 8 AM, the 1 PM boat (on Tuesday) may be your only choice. Keep in mind too that the ferry schedule is erratic, so confirm departure times with the tourist office to be sure you'll make it back to your ship on time. Round-trip fare is $8.

Exploring St. Kitts

Numbers in the margin correspond to points of interest on the St. Kitts map.

BASSETERRE

1 In the south of the island, **Basseterre,** St. Kitts's capital, is a walkable town. It's graced with tall palms, and although many of the buildings appear run-down and in need of paint, there are interesting shops, excellent art galleries, and some beautifully maintained houses.

The octagonal **Circus,** built in the style of London's famous Piccadilly Circus, has duty-free shops along the streets and courtyards off from it.

There are lovely gardens on the site of a former slave market at **Independence Square.** The square is surrounded on three sides by 18th-century Georgian buildings. *Off Bank St.*

St. George's Anglican Church, a handsome stone building with a crenellated tower, was built by the French in 1670. The British burned it down in 1706 and rebuilt it four years later, naming it after the patron saint of England. Since then, it has suffered fire, earthquake, and hurricanes, and was rebuilt in 1869. *Cayon St.*

Port Zante is an ambitious 27-acre cruise-ship pier/marina reclaimed from the sea. The domed welcome center sports an imposing neoclassical design with columns and stone arches. Plans for the structure (which sustained significant damage in a 1998 hurricane) include walkways, fountains, and West Indian–style buildings housing shops, restaurants, and perhaps even a hotel-casino. *Waterfront, behind the Circus.*

THE CARIBBEAN COAST

② **Old Road Town** was the first permanent English settlement in the West Indies, founded in 1624 by Thomas Warner. Take the side road toward the interior to find some Carib petroglyphs, testimony of even earlier habitation. The largest depicts a female figure, presumably a fertility goddess. *Main Rd., west of Challengers.*

③ The ruins of somewhat restored **Romney Manor** (it was destroyed by fire in 1996) and surrounding cottages that duplicate the old chattel-house style are set in 6 acres of gardens, with exotic flowers, an old bell tower, and an enormous gnarled 350-year-old saman tree. Inside, at Caribelle Batik (*see* Shopping, *below*), you can watch artisans hand-printing fabrics. Look for signs indicating a turnoff for Romney Manor near Old Road Town.

144

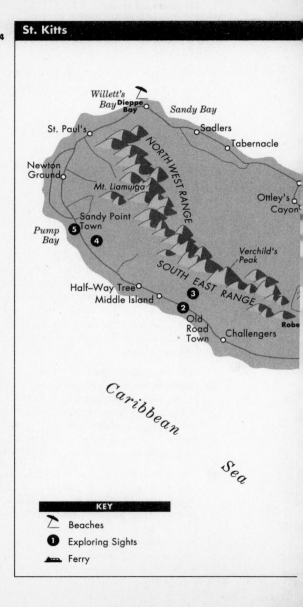

St. Kitts

Willett's Bay Dieppe Bay *Sandy Bay*
Sadlers
Tabernacle
St. Paul's
NORTH WEST RANGE
Newton Ground
Mt. Liamuiga
Ottley's Cayon
Sandy Point Town ❺ ❹
Pump Bay
Verchild's Peak
SOUTH EAST RANGE
Half-Way Tree
Middle Island ❸
❷
Old Road Town
Challengers
Robe

Caribbean Sea

KEY

⛱ Beaches

❶ Exploring Sights

⛴ Ferry

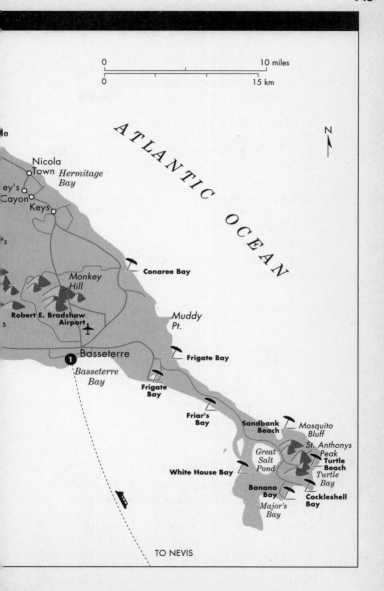

❹ The well-restored 38-acre fortress atop **Brimstone Hill** is part of a national park dedicated by Queen Elizabeth in 1985. From the parking area it's a steep walk up, but it's well worth it if military history and/or spectacular views interest you. The fort was erected by the English in 1690 and in the following century passed back and forth between the French and the English. A hurricane severely damaged the fortress in 1834, and in 1852 it was evacuated and dismantled. The citadel has been partially reconstructed. Nature trails snake through the tangle of surrounding hardwood forest and savanna—a fine spot to catch green vervet monkeys skittering about. *Main Rd., Brimstone Hill. Admission: $5. Open daily 9:30–5:30.*

❺ **Sandy Point Town,** a quaint village, contains West Indian–style raised cottages and a Roman Catholic church with stained-glass windows.

Exploring Nevis
Numbers in the margin correspond to points of interest on the Nevis map.

About 1,200 of the island's 9,300 inhabitants live in
❶ **Charlestown,** Nevis's capital. The town faces the Caribbean, about 12½ mi (20 km) south of Basseterre on St. Kitts. If you arrive by ferry, as most people do, you'll walk smack onto Main Street from the pier. Although it's true that tiny Charlestown, founded in 1660, has seen better times, it's easy to imagine how it must have looked in its heyday. The weathered buildings still have their fanciful galleries, elaborate gingerbread, wood shutters, and hanging plants.

The Georgian-style Alexander Hamilton Birthplace, which contains the **Museum of Nevis History,** is on the waterfront, covered in flora. *Low St., tel. 869/469–5786. Admission: $2. Open weekdays 9–4, Sat. 9–noon.*

❷ **Bath Springs** and the ruins of the Bath Hotel, built by John Huggins in 1778, sustained hurricane damage in 1995 and 1998, and the reopening has been delayed while the government lobbies the private sector to create a modernized spa. The springs, with temperatures of 104–108°F, bubble out of the hillside. Although locals still romp in the waters, you should think twice about it (not only are the springs dirty but they're closed, making such a romp technically illegal). Still, this is a fascinating sight. *Open weekdays 8–noon and 1–3:30, Sat. 8–noon.*

3 The **Nelson Museum** merits a visit for its memorabilia of Lord Nelson, including letters, documents, paintings, and even furniture from his flagship. Nelson was based in Antigua but came to Nevis often to court, and eventually to marry, Frances Nisbet, who lived on a 64-acre plantation here. *Bath Rd., tel. 869/469–0408. Admission: $2. Open weekdays 9–4, Sat. 9–noon.*

4 In addition to terraced gardens and arbors, the remarkable 7.8-acre **Nevis Botanical Gardens,** set in the glowering shadow of Mt. Nevis, have natural lagoons, streams, and waterfalls. You'll find a proper rose garden, a Rain Forest Conservatory, and a splendid re-creation of a plantation-style great house. *Montpelier Estate, tel. 869/469–3399. Admission: $8. Open daily 10–6.*

Shopping

Shops used to close for lunch from noon to 1, but more and more establishments are remaining open Monday–Saturday 8–4. Some shops close earlier on Thursday.

ST. KITTS

St. Kitts has limited shopping, but there are a few duty-free shops with good deals on jewelry, perfume, china, and crystal. Don't forget to pick up some CSR, a "new cane spirit drink" that's distilled from fresh sugarcane right on St. Kitts.

Most shopping plazas are in downtown Basseterre—try the **Palms Arcade,** on Fort Street near the Circus; the **Pelican Mall,** across the street from Port Zante (and which has a tourism office); and **Port Zante,** the cruise-ship pier, where construction of a shopping-dining complex is underway.

Kate Designs (Bank St., Basseterre, tel. 869/465–5265) showcases the enchanting silk works of Kate Spencer and the fanciful hats of Dale Isaacs. **Palm Crafts** (Palms Arcade, Basseterre, tel. 869/465–2599) sells savory Caribbean jams and jellies, resort wear by noted island designer John Warden, and hand-painted ceramics. **Spencer Cameron Art Gallery** (N. Independence Sq., Basseterre, tel. 869/465–1617) carries exceptional artwork by Caribbean artists, including the Carnival-inspired watercolors of Rosey Cameron. **Stonewall's**

Nevis

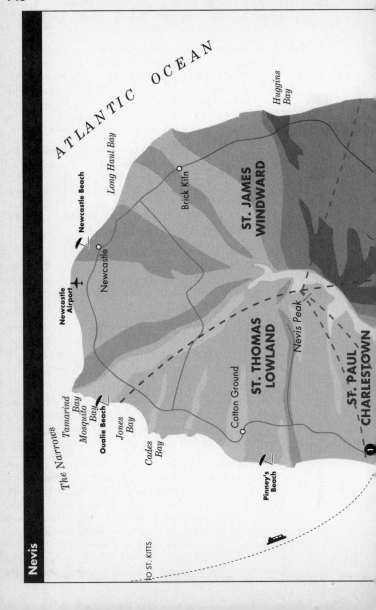

ATLANTIC OCEAN

Huggins Bay

Long Haul Bay

Brick Kiln

ST. JAMES WINDWARD

Newcastle Beach

Newcastle Airport

Newcastle

Tamarind Bay
Mosquito Bay
Oualie Beach

Jones Bay

Cades Bay

The Narrows

Cotton Ground

ST. THOMAS LOWLAND

Nevis Peak

ST. PAUL CHARLESTOWN

Pinney's Beach

1

TO ST. KITTS

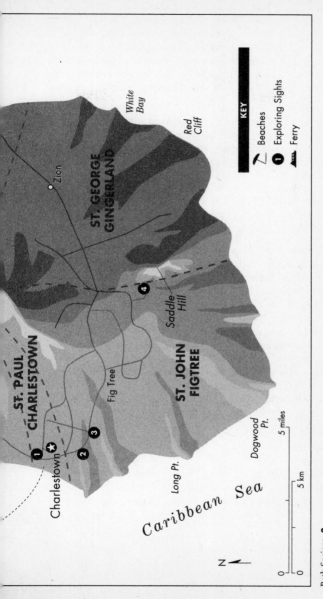

KEY

⅄ Beaches

❶ Exploring Sights

⛴ Ferry

White Bay

Red Cliff

ST. GEORGE GINGERLAND

○ Zion

❹

Saddle Hill

ST. PAUL CHARLESTOWN

Fig Tree

❶

★

❷ ❸

Charlestown

ST. JOHN FIGTREE

Long Pt.

Dogwood Pt.

0 |———| 5 miles

0 |———| 5 km

Caribbean Sea

N ↙

0

0

Bath Springs, **2**
Charlestown, **1**
Nelson
Museum, **3**
Nevis Botanical
Gardens, **4**

Tropical Boutique (7 Princes St., Basseterre, tel. 869/466–9124) carries top-notch products from around the Caribbean: handpainted Jamaican pottery, brass jewelry, resort wear, aromatherapy oils, and hot sauces. The works of **Caribelle Batik** (Romney Manor, tel. 869/465–6253) are well known; at the studio they sell wraps, T-shirts, dresses, and wall hangings.

NEVIS

Nevis is certainly not the place for a shopping spree, but there are some wonderful surprises, notably the island's stamps, fragrant honey, and batik and hand-embroidered clothing. Virtually all the shopping is concentrated on or just off Main Street in Charlestown, but there are two notable shopping arcades: the restored **Cotton Ginnery Complex** on the Charlestown waterfront, restored in 1997, which houses stalls of local artisans; and the new **Solomon's Arcade,** an upscale complex of local shops.

Caribco Gifts (Main St., Charlestown, tel. 869/469–1432) sells souvenirs emblazoned with Nevis logos. **Knickknacks** (between Main and Waterfront Sts. next to Unella's, Charlestown, tel. 869/469–5784) showcases works by local artisans. For dolls and baskets handcrafted in Nevis, visit the **Sandbox Tree** (Evelyn's Villa, Charlestown, tel. 869/469–5662). Among the offerings here are hand-painted chests. **Beach Works** (Pinney's Beach, inside the Beachcomber restaurant, tel. 869/469–0620) has become the island's classiest boutique, with an excellent selection of everything from bathing suits to Balinese batik and puppets. The **Eva Wilkin Gallery** (Clay Ghaut, Gingerland, tel. 869/469–2673), in the artist's light-filled former atelier, shows Wilkin's paintings, drawings, and prints.

Sports

GOLF

Duffers doff their hats to Nevis's impeccably maintained Robert Trent Jones Jr.–designed 18-hole, par 72, 6,766-yard championship course at the **Four Seasons** (tel. 869/469–1111). Greens fees are $75 for 9 holes; $125 for 18.

HIKING

Trails in the central mountains of St. Kitts vary from easy to don't-try-it-by-yourself. Monkey Hill and Verchild's Peak aren't difficult, although the Verchild's climb will take the better part of a day. Don't attempt Mt. Liamuiga without a guide. Tour rates range from $35 for a rain-forest walk to $65 for a volcano expedition. Addy of **Addy's Nature Tours** (tel. 869/465–8069) offers picnic lunch and cold drinks during treks through the rain forest; she also discusses island history and folklore. **Greg Pereira** (tel. 869/465–4121) takes groups on half-day trips into the rain forest and on full-day hikes up the volcano.

On Nevis, **Top to Bottom** (tel. 869/469–9080) offers eco-rambles (slower tours) and hikes that emphasize Nevis's volcanic and horticultural heritage. Three-hour rambles or hikes are $20 per person (snacks and juice included); it's $30 for a more strenuous climb up Mt. Nevis.

HORSEBACK RIDING
On St. Kitts, Wild North Frigate Bay and desolate Conaree Beach are great for riding. **Trinity Stable** (tel. 869/465–3226) guides will lead you into the hills at a leisurely gait.

On Nevis, you can take leisurely beach rides or tackle more demanding trail rides through the lush hills. You can arrange for both types of ride ($45 per person) and lessons ($20 per hour) through the **Nevis Equestrian Centre** (Pinney's Beach, near Cottonground, tel. 869/469–8118).

WATER SPORTS
St. Kitts has more than a dozen excellent dive sites. Auston MacLeod, a PADI-certified dive master–instructor and owner of **Pro-Divers** (tel. 869/465–3223), offers resort and certification courses. **Mr. X Watersports** (Frigate Bay, next to Monkey Bar, tel. 869/465–0673) arranges snorkeling trips ($35 per person), as well as waterskiing and sailing.

Beaches
The powdery white-sand beaches of St. Kitts, free and open to the public (even those occupied by hotels), are in the Frigate Bay area or on the lower peninsula. Two of the island's best are the twin beaches of **Banana Bay** and **Cockleshell Bay,** which cover more than 2 mi (3 km). Neither has food concessions or changing facilities; wear your bathing suit and bring a picnic lunch. Locals consider the southern side of **Friar's Bay** the island's finest beach. Here are changing rooms and dining options. **Turtle Beach,** at the south end of South East Peninsula Road, is perhaps the best

beach for cruise passengers. There's a good restaurant here with a water-sports concession (*see* Dining, *below*) and a great beach to laze on.

On Nevis, all the beaches are free to the public and there are no changing facilities, so wear a swimsuit under your clothes. **Oualie Beach,** just south of Mosquito Bay, is a beige-sand beach where the folks at Oualie Beach Hotel can mix you a drink and fix you up with water-sports equipment. The island's showpiece, **Pinney's Beach,** has almost 4 mi (6 km) of soft, golden sand on the calm Caribbean, lined with a magnificent grove of palm trees. There's a good place for lunch here, too (*see* Dining, *below*).

Dining
Restaurants occasionally add a 10% service charge to your bill; ask if it isn't printed on the menu. When there's no service charge, a tip of 15% is appropriate.

ST. KITTS

$$$ **Rawlins Plantation.** If you want to experience the civility of one of the 18th-century great house inns for which St. Kitts and Nevis are famed, repair to this lovely dining room, with fieldstone walls, antique furnishings, and high vaulted ceilings. Co-owner Claire Rawson oversees the bountiful authentic West Indian lunch buffet ($25), including such dishes as flying-fish fritters, breadfruit salad, and *bobote* (eggplant, ground beef, spices, curry, and homemade chutney). It's worth the long ride, and you can visit artist Kate Spencer's atelier on the adjoining grounds. *St. Paul's, tel. 869/465–6221. Reservations essential. AE, MC, V.*

$–$$ **Ballahoo.** This second-floor terrace restaurant, in the heart of downtown, draws a crowd for breakfast, lunch, and dinner. Lilting calypso and reggae on the sound system, whirring ceiling fans, and colorful prints create the appropriate tropical ambience. Specialties include conch simmered in garlic butter, lobster stir fry, and (it's true) a rum-and-banana toasted sandwich. At lunchtime the prices for many dishes are slashed nearly in half. *Fort St., Basseterre, tel. 869/465–4197. AE, MC, V. Closed Sun.*

$–$$ **Turtle Beach Bar and Grill.** An alluring beach setting, simple but scrumptious cuisine (including grilled lobster, honey-mustard ribs, and coconut shrimp salad), and numerous activities make this restaurant a perfect place to while away the day. You can snorkel; spot monkeys and hawksbill turtles; laze in a hammock; rent a kayak, Windsurfer, or mountain bike; even go deep-sea fishing. The owners can arrange a water taxi ($20–$25 each way) to take you to Nevis, just 15 minutes away. *Turtle Beach (south end of South East Peninsula Rd.), tel. 869/469–8069. AE, MC, V.*

NEVIS

$$$ Golden Rock. Tables are draped in pink and arranged in a romantic setting. Enchanting Eva Wilkin originals grace the walls, and straw mats and unglazed local pottery add to the island ambience. Local Nevisian cuisine is the specialty here; velvety pumpkin soup, grilled local snapper with *tania* (a type of tuber) fritters, and green papaya pie are house favorites. *Gingerland, tel. 869/469–3346. Reservations essential. AE, MC, V. Closed Sun.*

$ SunShine's. Everything about this palm-thatched beach shack is colorful and larger-than-life, including the Rasta man SunShine himself. Picnic tables and palm trees alike are splashed with bright Rasta sunrise-to-sunset colors. Fishermen cruise up to the grill with their catch; you might savor lobster rolls, conch fritters, or snapper Creole. Try the lethal house specialty, the Killer Bee rum punch. *Pinney's Beach, tel. 869/469–5817. No credit cards.*

$ Unella's. The atmosphere is nothing fancy—just tables on a second-floor porch on the waterfront—but the fare is good West Indian. Stop here for exceptional lobster, curried lamb, spareribs, and steamed conch. *Waterfront, Charlestown, tel. 869/469–5574. No credit cards.*

St. Lucia

Rugged St. Lucia—with towering mountains, dense rain forest, fertile green valleys, and acres of banana plantations—lies in the middle of the Windward Islands. Nicknamed "the Helen of the West Indies" because of its natural beauty, St. Lucia is distinguished from its neighbors by its geological sites. The Pitons, twin peaks on the southwest coast that have become a symbol of this island, soar nearly 1 km (½ mi) above the ocean floor. Nearby, outside the French colonial town of Soufrière, are a "drive-in" volcano and bubbling sulfur springs with curative waters that have rejuvenated bathers for nearly three centuries.

A century and a half of battles between the French and English resulted in St. Lucia's changing hands 14 times before 1814, when England ultimately won possession. In 1979 the island became an independent state within the British Commonwealth of Nations. The official language is English, although most people also speak a French Creole patois.

Currency

St. Lucia uses the Eastern Caribbean (E.C.) dollar. The exchange rate is about EC$2.70 to US$1. Although U.S. dollars are readily accepted, you'll often get change in E.C. currency. Major credit cards and traveler's checks are also widely accepted. All prices given below are in U.S. dollars unless otherwise indicated.

Telephones

You can dial international numbers directly from St. Lucia's pay phones and card phones. Telephone services are available at Pointe Seraphine, the cruise-ship port of entry. To charge an overseas call to a major credit card, dial 811; there's no surcharge.

Shore Excursions

The following is a good choice in St. Lucia. It may not be offered by all cruise lines. Time and price are approximate.

NATURAL BEAUTY

La Soufrière and the Pitons. Travel the mountainous and winding West Coast Road for a spectacular view of the Pitons on the way to La Soufrière volcano and the sulfur springs, nearby Diamond Falls and Mineral Baths, and the Botanical Gardens. Travel may be by a combination of catamaran, bus, and minivan. *6–8 hrs. Cost: $70.*

Coming Ashore

Most cruise ships call at the capital city of Castries, on the island's northwest coast. Either of two docking areas are used: Pointe Seraphine, a port of entry and duty-free shopping complex, or Port Castries, a commercial dock across the harbor. Ferry service connects the two docking areas.

Smaller vessels call at Soufrière, on the island's southwest coast. Ships calling at Soufrière usually anchor offshore and tender passengers to the wharf.

Finally, a travel companion that doesn't snore on the plane or eat all your peanuts.

When traveling, your MCI WorldCom Card is the best way to keep in touch. Our operators speak your language, so they'll be able to connect you back home—no matter where your travels take you. Plus, your MCI WorldCom Card is easy to use, and even earns you frequent flyer miles every time you use it. When you add in our great rates, you get something even more valuable: peace-of-mind. So go ahead. Travel the world. MCI WorldCom just brought it a whole lot closer.

You can even sign up today at www.mci.com/worldphone or ask your operator to make a collect call to 1-410-314-2938.

EASY TO CALL WORLDWIDE

1 **Just dial the WorldPhone access number of the country you're calling from.**
2 **Dial or give the operator your MCI WorldCom Card number.**
3 **Dial or give the number you're calling.**

Aruba	800-888-8
Bahamas/Bermuda	1-800-888-8000
British Virgin Islands	1-800-888-8000
China	
Available from most major cities	108-12
For a Mandarin-speaking Operator	108-17
Costa Rica ◆	0-800-012-2222
Japan ◆	
To call using JT	0044-11-121
To call using KDD	00539-121▶
To call using IDC	0066-55-121

For your complete WorldPhone calling guide, dial the WorldPhone access number for the country you're in and ask the operator for Customer Service. In the U.S. call 1-800-431-5402.

◆ Public phones may require deposit of coin or phone card for dial tone.
▶ Regulation does not permit Intra-Japan calls.

EARN FREQUENT FLYER MILES

American Airlines®
AAdvantage®

Continental Airlines
OnePass®

▲ Delta Air Lines
SkyMiles®

▥ MILEAGE PLUS®
United Airlines

US AIRWAYS
DIVIDEND MILES

MCI WorldCom, its logo and the names of the products referred to herein are proprietary marks of MCI WorldCom, Inc. All airline names and logos are proprietary marks of the respective airlines. All airline program rules and conditions apply.

Tourist information offices are at Pointe Seraphine in Castries and along the waterfront on Bay Street in Soufrière. Downtown Castries is within walking distance of the pier, and the produce market and adjacent craft and vendor's markets are the main attractions. Soufrière is a sleepy West Indian town, but it's worth a short walk around the central square to view the authentic French colonial architecture. Most of St. Lucia's sightseeing is near Soufrière.

You can hire a taxi at the docks. Cabs are unmetered, but the government has issued a list of standard fares that are posted at the entrance to Pointe Seraphine. A 10- to 20-minute ride north from Pointe Seraphine to Reduit Beach and Rodney Bay should cost about $16. For sightseeing trips to Soufrière, at least a 1½-hour drive south, expect to pay $20 per hour for up to four people and plan an excursion of 6–8 hours, including lunch. Whatever your destination, negotiate the price with the driver before you depart—and be sure that you both understand whether the rate is in E.C. or U.S. dollars. Drivers appreciate a 10% tip.

Exploring St. Lucia

Numbers in the margin correspond to points of interest on the St. Lucia map.

CASTRIES AREA

❶ The **Castries Market** is at the corner of Jeremie and Peynier streets, just steps from the harbor. It's a typical, colorful, West Indian, open-air market—although a good portion is now covered by bright orange roofs as protection from the hot sun and occasional rain shower. The market is open every day but liveliest on Saturday morning, when farm wives come to sell their produce. Next door is the craft market, where you can buy pottery, wood carvings, and handwoven straw items. Across Peynier Street, at the Vendor's Arcade, you can buy souvenirs and handicrafts.

❷ **Derek Walcott Square** is a block of green oasis in downtown Castries, bordered by Brazil, Laborie, Micoud, and Bourbon streets. Formerly Columbus Square, it was renamed for the hometown poet who won the 1992 Nobel Prize in Literature. On the Laborie Street side of the square is a huge tree estimated to be 400 years old.

St. Lucia

KEY

🏖 Beaches
⚓ Cruise Ship Terminal
➊ Exploring Sights
🌲 Rain Forest

St. Lucia Channel — *Cap Pt.*
Pigeon Pt. ➍
Rodney Bay
Reduit Beach ➌
Gros Islet
Anse Lavouette
Esperance Harbour
Cape Marquis
Vigie Beach
Ptd. Seraphine
Castries Harbour
George F. L. Charles (Vigie) Airport
➊ ➋
Castries ★
Morne Fortune ➎
Grand Anse Bay
Grande Anse
La Sorcière
Caribbean Sea
Grande Cul de Sac Bay
Marigot Bay
Marigot Beach
Roseau
Anse-la-Raye
Fond d'or Bay
Dennery
Grande Caille Pt.
Canaries
Anse Cochon
Praslin Bay
Soufrière
Anse Chastanet
➏ ➐
Soufrière Harbour
Fond St. Jacques
➑
➓ ➒
Petit Piton
Gros Piton
Micoud
Vierge Pt.
Gros Piton Pt.
Choiseul
Laborie
Hewanorra International Airport
Savannes Bay
Laborie Bay
Vieux Fort
Vieux Fort
Maria Islands
Honeymoon Beach
Anse de Sables
Moule à Chique Peninsula

ATLANTIC OCEAN

N

0 — 4 miles
0 — 6 km

Next to the square, the Roman Catholic **Cathedral of the Immaculate Conception,** built in 1897, looks rather somber from the outside; inside, the walls are decorated with colorful murals reworked in 1985 by St. Lucian artist Dunstan St. Omer. *Facing Brazil St., downtown Castries.*

3 **Rodney Bay,** about 11 km (7 mi) north of Castries, is one of the Caribbean's busiest marinas. Reduit Beach, a fine strip of white sand with a water-sports center (at the Rex St. Lucian Hotel), is also here. Several good lunch spots are within walking distance of the beach and/or marina.

4 According to island tales, pirate Jambe de Bois (Wooden Leg) used **Pigeon Island,** off St. Lucia's northern tip, as his hideout. Now a national park, Pigeon Island has a beach, restaurants, picnic areas, and calm waters for swimming. On the grounds you'll see ruins of barracks, batteries, and garrisons from the French and British battles for control of St. Lucia. An excellent small museum has interactive and historical exhibits. *St. Lucia National Trust, tel. 758/450–8167. Admission: $4. Open daily 9–5.*

5 Heading south from Castries, a corkscrew road climbs up **Morne Fortune** ("Hill of Good Luck"). You'll pass beautiful tropical foliage and flowers—frangipani, lilies, bougainvillea, hibiscus, and oleander—and get a splendid panoramic view of the city and harbor.

Ft. Charlotte, on the Morne, was begun in 1764 by the French as the Citadelle du Morne Fortune and completed and renamed by the British after 20 years of battling and changing hands. Its old barracks and batteries have been converted to government buildings, but you can view the remains— redoubts, a guardroom, stables, and cells.

SOUFRIÈRE AREA

6 It's a 1½-hour drive on the winding West Coast Road from Castries to **Soufrière,** the French colonial capital named for the nearby volcano. The mountainous region of St. Lucia is breathtakingly lush, and the road that snakes along the coast offers spectacular views of the Pitons, the rain forest, small bays and villages, and the Caribbean Sea. The town itself is small but charming in its authenticity, with architecture that dates back to the colonial period.

❼ The splendid **Diamond Botanical Gardens** has specimen tropical flowers and trees growing in their natural habitat. A pathway leads to Diamond Waterfall, where the mineral-rich cascade has created a multihued effect on the river rocks. You can slip into your swimsuit and take a dip in the mineral baths. *Soufrière Estate, tel. 758/452–4759. Admission: $2.75 (gardens); baths: $2.50 (outdoor), $3.75 (private). Open weekdays 10–5; Sun. and holidays 10–3.*

❽ **La Soufrière,** the "drive-in" volcano, is southeast of the town of Soufrière. More than 20 black, belching, sometimes smelly, sulfurous pools bubble, bake, and steam on the surface of this natural wonder. *Bay St., tel. 758/459–5500. Admission: $1.25, includes tour. Open daily 9–5.*

❾ **Morne Coubaril Estate** is an historic 250-acre coconut and cocoa plantation that dates back to 1713. It still produces copra, manioc flour, and chocolate but mainly operates as a museum. On a 90-minute eco-tour, guides explain 18th-century plantation life and you explore a reconstructed village. A Creole buffet lunch is served ($10) by reservation only. *Soufrière, tel. 758/459–7340. Admission: $6, includes tour. Open daily 9–5.*

❿ **The Pitons** have become the symbol of St. Lucia. These unusual pyramidal cones, covered with thick tropical vegetation, rise precipitously out of the cobalt sea just south of Soufrière Bay. Petit Piton (2,619 ft) is taller than Gros Piton (2,461 ft), though Gros is, as the word translates, broader. This area is wonderfully scenic.

Shopping

Local products include silk-screened or batik fabric and clothing, pottery, wood carvings, cocoa and spices, and baskets. The only duty-free shopping is at Pointe Seraphine or La Place Carenage, both on the harborside. You'll want to experience the **Castries Market** and scour the adjacent **Vendor's Arcade** and **Craft Market** for handicrafts and souvenirs at bargain prices (*see* Exploring St. Lucia, *above*).

Artsibit Gallery (Brazil and Mongiraud Sts., Castries, tel. 758/452–7865) sells the work of top St. Lucian painters and sculptors. **Bagshaw Studios** (La Toc Rd., La Toc Bay, tel. 758/452–2139 or 758/451–9249) sells clothing and household items created from silk-screened and hand-printed fabrics designed by Stanley Bagshaw. You'll also find a Bagshaw boutique at Pointe Seraphine. **Caribelle Batik** (37 Old Victoria Rd., Morne Fortune, tel. 758/452–3785) welcomes visitors to watch artisans creating batik clothing and wall hangings.

Eudovic Art Studio (Morne Fortune, tel. 758/452–2747), 15 minutes south of Castries, sells trays, masks, and figures that are carved in the studio from native mahogany, red cedar, and eucalyptus wood. **Made in St. Lucia** (Gablewoods Mall, north of Castries, tel. 758/453–2788) sells only items made on the island—sandals, shirts, hot sauces, costume jewelry, carved wooden items, clay coal pots for cooking, original art, and more—all at reasonable prices. **Noah's Arkade** (Jeremie St., Castries, tel. 758/452–2523; Pointe Seraphine, tel. 758/452–7488) has hammocks, straw mats, baskets, and carvings, as well as island books and maps.

Pointe Seraphine, the cruise-ship terminal, is a modern, Spanish-style complex where more than 20 shops sell typical duty-free goods; to get the duty-free price, you must show your boarding pass or cabin key. Native crafts are also sold here. **La Place Carenage,** smaller than Pointe Seraphine but with many of the same shops, is on the opposite side of Castries Harbour.

Soufrière is not much of a shopping port, although there's a small arts and crafts center on the wharf.

Sports

FISHING

Among the sea creatures in these waters are dolphinfish, Spanish mackerel, barracuda, kingfish, sailfish, and white marlin. For half-day excursions, contact **Captain Mike's** (Vigie Cove Marina, Castries, tel. 758/452–7044) or **Mako Watersports** (Rodney Bay Marina, tel. 758/452–0412).

GOLF

Golf courses on St. Lucia are scenic and good fun, but they're not quite world-class. **St. Lucia Golf and Country Club** (Cap Estate, tel. 758/452–8523) is a 9-hole public course that can be played as 18. A $49.50 package includes 18 holes of golf, cart, and club rental. Reservations are essential.

HIKING

St. Lucia is laced with trails, but you should not attempt
the remote ones on your own. The **Forest and Land Department** (tel. 758/450–2231) has established trails throughout the rain forest and can provide a guide for $10 per
person. The **St. Lucia National Trust** (tel. 758/452–5005)
maintains two hiking trails: one is at Anse La Liberté, near
Canaries on the Caribbean coast, and the other is in the
east, on the Atlantic coast, from Mandélé to the Fregate
Islands Nature Reserve. Full-day excursions, including
lunch, cost about $40 per person. **Pigeon Island** is a good
place for an informal hike or a brisk walk.

HORSEBACK RIDING

For trail rides in the north, contact **International Riding Stables** (Beauséjour Estate, Gros Islet, tel. 758/452–8139) or
Trim's Riding School (Cas-en-Bas, Gros Islet, tel. 758/452–
8273). Prices start at about $35 for a one-hour ride.

SCUBA DIVING

The coral reefs at Anse Cochon and Anse Chastanet, on
the southwest coast, are popular beach-entry dive sites. In
the north, Pigeon Island is the most convenient site. For excursion information, contact **Scuba St. Lucia** (Anse Chastanet, Soufrière, tel. 758/459–7000; Rex St. Lucian, Rodney
Bay, tel. 758/459–7755); **Dolphin Divers** (Rodney Bay Marina, tel. 758/452–9485); and **Frogs** (Windjammer Landing, Labrelotte Bay, tel. 758/452–0913; Jalousie Hilton,
Soufrière, tel. 758/459–7666, ext. 4024).

TENNIS

St. Lucia Racquet Club (Club St. Lucia, Cap Estate, tel. 758/
450–0551) is one of the top tennis facilities in the Caribbean.
It has nine courts and charges $10 per person per hour for
use of the facilities; reservations are required.

Beaches

All of St. Lucia's beaches are open to the public, but resorts are sometimes less than welcoming to large groups
of cruise-ship passengers. A good alternative for picnick-
ing and swimming is **Pigeon Island,** admission $4. It has
a white-sand beach and a small restaurant and is about a
30-minute drive from Pointe Seraphine. **Reduit Beach,** 20

minutes north of Castries and adjacent to Rodney Bay, is probably St. Lucia's best beach. Water-sports equipment can be rented at the Rex St. Lucian hotel. Near Soufrière, **Anse Chastanet** is a gray-sand beach with a backdrop of green mountains, a view of the Pitons, and the island's best reefs for snorkeling and diving. A dive shop, restaurant, and bar are on the beach.

Dining

An 8% government tax is applicable to your bill, and most restaurants add a 10% service charge in lieu of tip.

$$$ **Dasheene Restaurant and Bar.** The breathtaking view—the Pitons look close enough to touch—plus some of the best food on St. Lucia are reasons to stop at this open-air perch high in the mountains. Fresh-caught fish is always worthwhile, but there are also inspired salads and sandwiches on the luncheon menu. *Ladera Resort, Soufrière, tel. 758/459–7323. AE, DC, MC, V.*

$$–$$$ **Jimmie's.** This open-air mom-and-pop place is five minutes from the ship (via taxi), and worth it for the great views. Popular with locals as well as visitors, Jimmie's specializes in seafood—from Creole stuffed crab for an appetizer to the special seafood platter for an entrée. Dessert lovers had better be in a banana mood—everything is made with St. Lucian "figs." *Vigie Cove Marina, Castries, tel. 758/452–5142. Reservations not accepted. AE, MC, V.*

$$ **Hummingbird Restaurant.** On the north side of town, within walking distance of the wharf, is this cheerful waterfront restaurant and bar. The chef creates delicious French creole cuisine using fresh seafood or chicken, local herbs, and fresh vegetables. Sandwiches and salads are also available. After lunch, be sure to stop in at the proprietor's batik studio. *Hummingbird Beach Resort, Soufrière, tel. 758/459–7232. AE, D, MC, V.*

$$ **The Still.** This attractive restaurant is a popular stop en route to Diamond Falls and La Soufrière volcano. The emphasis is on Creole cuisine, using local vegetables—christophenes, breadfruits, yams, callaloo—and seafood, but you'll also find pork and beef dishes on the menu. All produce used here is grown organically on the estate. *Still Plantation, Bay St., Soufrière, tel. 758/459–7224. MC, V.*

St. Martin/St. Maarten

St. Martin/St. Maarten: one tiny island, just 59 square km (37 square mi), with two different accents, and ruled by two sovereign nations. Here French and Dutch have lived side by side for hundreds of years, and when you cross from one country to the next there are no border patrols, no customs. In fact, the only indication that you have crossed a border at all is a small sign and a change in road surface.

St. Martin/St. Maarten epitomizes tourist islands in the sun, where services are well developed but there's still some Caribbean flavor left. The Dutch side is ideal for people who like plenty to do. The French side has a more genteel ambience, more fashionable shopping, and a Continental flair. The combination makes an almost ideal port. On the negative side, the island has been completely developed. There's gambling, but table limits are so low that high rollers will have a better time gamboling on the beach. It can be fun to shop, and you'll find an occasional bargain, but many goods are cheaper in the United States.

Though Dutch is the official language of St. Maarten, and French of St. Martin, almost everyone speaks English. If you hear a language you can't quite place, it's Papiamento, a Spanish-based Creole.

Currency

Legal tender on the Dutch side is the Netherlands Antilles florin (guilder), written NAf; on the French side, it's the French franc (F). In general, the exchange rate is about NAf1.80 to US$1, and 5.65F to US$1. There's little need to exchange money, though, as dollars are accepted everywhere. All prices given below are in U.S. dollars unless otherwise indicated.

Telephones

To phone from the Dutch side to the French side, dial 00–590 plus the local number. From the French side to the Dutch side, dial 00–5995 plus the local number. Remember that a call from one side to the other is an international call.

At the Landsradio in Philipsburg, St. Maarten, there are facilities for overseas calls and an AT&T USADirect telephone. On the French side, it's not possible to make collect calls to the United States, but you can make credit-card calls from a phone on the side of the tourist office in Marigot. The operator will assign you a PIN number, valid for as long as you specify. Calls to the United States are about $4 per minute. To call from other public phones, you'll need to go to Marigot's post office and buy a télécarte.

Shore Excursions

The following is a good choice in St. Martin/St. Maarten. It may not be offered by all cruise lines. Times and prices are approximate.

UNDERSEA CREATURES

Orient Beach Sojourn. Take a short bus ride to beautiful Baie Orientale (Orient Bay Beach) on the French side of the island. The 1½-mi beach is often referred to as the French Riviera of the Caribbean, with its trendy, chic beachside restaurants and bars and colorful chaises longues and umbrellas. Lunch and drinks are included. *4½ hrs. Cost: $45.*

Coming Ashore

Most cruise ships drop anchor off the Dutch capital of Philipsburg or dock in the marina at the southern tip of the Philipsburg harbor. If your ship anchors, tenders will ferry you to the town pier in the middle of town, where taxis await passengers. If your ship docks at the marina, downtown is a 15-minute taxi ride away. The walk is not recommended. To get to major sights outside of Philipsburg or Marigot, your best bet is a tour via taxi; negotiate the rate before you get in. A 2½-hour to 3-hour tour of the island for two people should be about $30, plus $10 per additional person. Nowhere on the island is more than a 30-minute drive from Marigot or Philipsburg.

Taxis are government-regulated and costly. Authorized taxis display stickers of the St. Maarten Taxi Association. Taxis are also available at Marigot.

Exploring St. Martin/St. Maarten

Numbers in the margin correspond to points of interest on the St. Martin/St. Maarten map.

THE DUTCH SIDE

❶ Philipsburg, the Dutch capital of St. Maarten, stretches about 1½ km (1 mi) along an isthmus between Great Bay

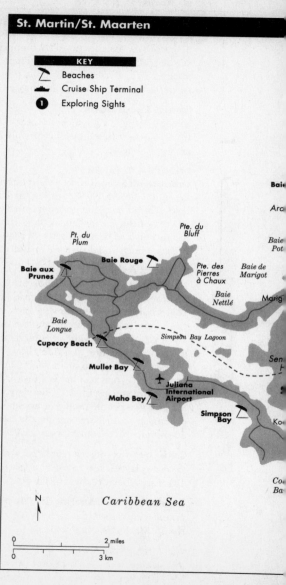

St. Martin/St. Maarten

KEY

⛱ Beaches

⛴ Cruise Ship Terminal

❶ Exploring Sights

Baie

Ara

Baie
Pot

Pt. du
Plum

Pte. du
Bluff

Baie Rouge ⛱

Pte. des
Pierres
à Chaux

Baie de
Marigot

**Baie aux
Prunes** ⛱

Baie
Nettlé

Marig

Baie
Longue

Simpson Bay Lagoon

Cupecoy Beach ⛱

Mullet Bay ⛱

Sen
H

✈ Juliana
International
Airport

Maho Bay ⛱

**Simpson
Bay** ⛱

Ko

N

Caribbean Sea

Co
Ba

0 ———— 2 miles
0 ———— 3 km

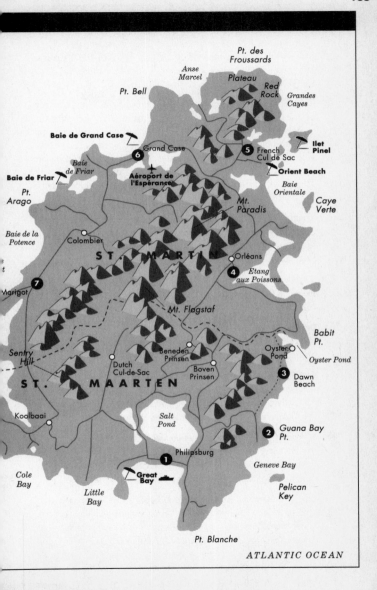

Pt. des
Froussards

Anse
Marcel

Plateau

Red
Rock

Grandes
Cayes

Pt. Bell

Baie de Grand Case

Grand Case

6

5 French
Cul de Sac

**Ilet
Pinel**

Baie
de Friar

Orient Beach

Baie de Friar

**Aéroport de
l'Espérance**

Baie
Orientale

Pt.
Arago

Caye
Verte

Mt.
Paradis

Baie de la
Potence

Colombier

S T .   M A R T I N

Orléans

4 Etang
aux Poissons

Marigot

7

Mt. Flagstaf

Babit
Pt.

Sentry
Hill

Beneden
Prinsen

Oyster
Pond

Oyster Pond

Dutch
Cul-de-Sac

Boven
Prinsen

3 Dawn
Beach

S T .   M A A R T E N

Koolbaai

Salt
Pond

2 Guana Bay
Pt.

1 Philipsburg

Geneve Bay

Cole
Bay

**Great
Bay**

Pelican
Key

Little
Bay

Pt. Blanche

ATLANTIC OCEAN

and Salt Pond and is easily explored on foot. It has three parallel streets: Front Street, Back Street, and Pond Fill. Little lanes called *steegjes* connect Front Street with Back Street, which is considerably less congested because it has fewer shops. A walk from one end of downtown to the other takes half an hour, even if you stop at a couple of stores.

The first stop for cruise passengers should be Wathey Square (pronounced watty), in the middle of the isthmus, which bustles with vendors, souvenir shops, and tourists. The streets to the right and left are lined with hotels, duty-free shops, restaurants, and cafés, most in West Indian cottages decorated in pastels with gingerbread trim. Narrow alleyways lead to arcades and flower-filled courtyards with yet more boutiques and eateries.

To explore beyond Philipsburg, start at the west end of Front Street. The road (which becomes Sucker Garden Road) leads north along Salt Pond and begins to climb and curve just outside town.

② The first right off Sucker Garden Road leads to **Guana Bay Point,** which gives you a splendid view of the east coast, tiny deserted islands, and little St. Barts in the distance.

③ **Dawn Beach,** an excellent snorkeling beach, lies on the east coast of the island, just below Oyster Pond, and has an active sailing community.

THE FRENCH SIDE

Cruise-ship passengers following the main road north out of Philipsburg will come first to Orléans. This settlement,
④ also known as the **French Quarter,** is the island's oldest.

⑤ North of Orléans is the **French Cul de Sac,** where you'll see the French colonial mansion of St. Martin's mayor nestled in the hills. From here the road swirls south through green hills and pastures, past flower-entwined stone fences.

Past the airport, Aéroport de L'Espérance, is the town of
⑥ **Grand Case,** known as the "Restaurant Capital of the Caribbean." Along its 1½-km-long (1-mi-long) main street are more than 20 restaurants serving French, Italian, Indonesian, and Vietnamese fare, as well as fresh seafood. Along the shore, vendors known as *lolos* sell delicious barbecued chicken, beef on skewers, and other delicacies.

❼ The capital of the French side is **Marigot.** (If you're coming from Grand Case, follow the signs south to rue de la République.) Marina Port La Royale is the shopping complex at the port; rue de la République and rue de la Liberté, which border the bay, are also filled with duty-free shops, boutiques, and bistros. The road south from Marigot leads to the official border, where a simple marker, placed here in 1948, commemorates 300 years of peaceful coexistence. This road will bring you back to Philipsburg.

Shopping

Prices can be 25%–50% below those in the United States and Canada for French perfume, liquor, cognac and fine liqueurs, leather, Swiss watches, and other luxury items. However, it pays to know the prices back home; not all goods are a bargain. Although most merchants are reputable, there are occasional reports of inferior or fake merchandise passed off as the real thing—in particular, inferior cigars are sometimes passed off as genuine Havanas. When vendors bargain excessively, their wares are often suspect.

In Philipsburg, **Front Street** is one long strip of boutiques and shops; **Old Street,** near the end of Front Street, is packed with stores, boutiques, and open-air cafés. At Philipsburg's **Shipwreck Shop,** look for Caribelle batiks, hammocks, handmade jewelry, the local guava-berry liqueur, and herbs and spices. You'll find almost 100 boutiques in the **Mullet Bay** and **Maho** shopping plazas. In general, you'll find smarter fashions in Marigot than in Philipsburg. In Marigot, wrought-iron balconies, colorful awnings, and gingerbread trim decorate the shops and tiny boutiques in the **Marina Port La Royale** and on the main streets, **rue de la Liberté** and **rue de la République.**

Sports

FISHING

In Philipsburg, contact **Bobby's Marina** (tel. 599/5–22366) for information on fishing charters.

GOLF

Mullet Bay Resort (tel. 599/5–52801) has an 18-hole championship course. The greens fee is $108 ($26 club rental) for 18 holes and $62 ($21 club rental) for 9 holes.

WATER SPORTS

Certified dive centers offer scuba instruction, rentals, and trips. On the Dutch side, try **Trade Winds Dive Center** (tel. 599/5–75176) and **St. Maarten Divers** (tel. 599/5–22446). On the French side, there's **Lou Scuba** (tel. 590/87–16– 61) and **Blue Ocean** (tel. 590/87–89–73), both PADI-certified. You can rent boats at **Caraibes Sport Boats** (tel. 590/87–89–38) and **Caribbean Watersports** (tel. 590/87–58–66).

Beaches

The island's 16 km (10 mi) of beaches are all open to cruise-ship passengers. On beaches owned by resorts, you might be charged a small fee (about $3) for access to changing facilities. Water-sports equipment can be rented at most hotels. Topless bathing is common on the French side. If you take a cab to a remote beach, be sure to arrange a specific time for the driver to return for you. Don't leave valuables unattended on the beach.

Baie Longue, on the French side, is the island's best beach. The 1½-km-long (1-mi-long) curve of white sand at the island's western tip offers excellent snorkeling and swimming but no facilities. **Baie Orientale** (the beach at Orient Bay) is the island's best-known clothing-optional beach. The nude section is to the right on the southern end. This is windsurfing heaven, with a couple of on-site rental shops that enable you to take advantage of the steady trade winds. The beach at **Baie de Friar** (Friar's Bay) is on a small cove between Marigot and Grand Case. It attracts a casual crowd of locals, and has a small snack bar. **Cupecoy Beach,** near the Dutch–French border (on the Dutch side), is a narrower, more secluded curve of white sand. There are no facilities, but vendors sell drinks and rent beach chairs and umbrellas. This is a clothing-optional beach.

Dining

Restaurants on the French side often figure a service charge into the menu prices. On the Dutch side, most restaurants add 10%–15% to the bill. You can, if so moved by exceptional service, leave a tip.

$$$ **La Vie en Rose.** This bustling restaurant is right off the pier, a 30-second stroll from the tourist office. The menu is classic French with an occasional Caribbean twist—fillet of swordfish sautéed in a passion fruit–butter sauce, freshwater crayfish in puff pastry. Save room for chocolate mousse cake topped with vanilla sauce. The ground-floor tearoom and pastry shop serve an excellent luncheon with wine for about $20. *Rue de la République and bd. de France, Marigot, St. Martin, tel. 590/87–54–42. AE, D, DC, MC, V. Reservations essential in season. No lunch Sun.*

$–$$$ Mini-Club. This upstairs restaurant on the harbor in Marigot serves terrific Creole and French cuisine. The chairs and madras tablecloths are sun-yellow and orange, and the whole thing is built, tree house–like, around the trunks of coconut trees. *Front de Mer, Marigot, St. Martin, tel. 590/87–50–69. AE, MC, V. No lunch Sun.*

$–$$ Chesterfield's. Casual lunches of burgers and salads are served at this marina restaurant. Specialties include French onion soup and shrimp. The Mermaid Bar is popular with yachtsmen. *Great Bay Marina, Philipsburg, St. Maarten, tel. 599/5–23484. D, MC, V.*

$–$$ Shiv Sagar. Authentic East Indian cuisine, emphasizing Kashmiri and Mogul specialties, is served in this small, mirrored room fragrant with cumin and coriander. Marvelous tandooris and curries are offered, but try one of the less-familiar preparations such as *madrasi machi* (red snapper cooked in a blend of hot spices). A large selection of vegetarian dishes is also offered. *20 Front St., Philipsburg, St. Maarten, tel. 599/5–22299. AE, D, DC, MC, V. Closed Sun.*

St. Thomas and St. John

St. Thomas is the busiest cruise port of call in the world. As many as eight ships may visit in a single day. Don't expect an exotic island experience: one of the three U.S.Virgin Islands (with St. Croix and St. John), St. Thomas is as American as any place on the mainland, complete with McDonald's franchises and HBO. The positive side of all this development is that there are more tours here than anywhere else in the Caribbean, and every year the excursions get better. Of course, shopping is the big draw in Charlotte Amalie, but experienced travelers remember the days of "real" bargains. Today, so many passengers fill the stores that it's a seller's market. One of St. Thomas's best tourist attractions is its neighboring island, St. John, with its beautiful Virgin Islands National Park and beaches.

Currency

The U.S. dollar is the official currency of St. Thomas and St. John.

Telephones

It's as easy to call home from St. Thomas and St. John as from any city in the United States. On St. Thomas, public phones are easily found, and AT&T has a telecommunications center across from the Havensight Mall (*see* Coming Ashore, *below*). On St. John public phones are in front of the U.S. Post Office, east of the tender landing and at the ferry dock.

Shore Excursions

The following are good choices on St. Thomas and St. John. They may not be offered by all cruise lines. Times and prices are approximate.

ADVENTURE

Helicopter Tour. If you haven't taken a helicopter tour before, sign up for this exciting aerial tour of St. Thomas and surrounding islands. *1½ hrs, includes 40-min flight time. Cost: $99.*

NATURAL BEAUTY

St. John Island Tour. Either your ship tenders you in to St. John in the morning before docking at St. Thomas, or you take a bus from the St. Thomas docks to the St. John ferry. On St. John, an open-air safari bus winds through the national park to a beach for snorkeling, swimming, and sunbathing. (If you have the option, go to any beach but Trunk Bay.) *4½ hrs. Cost: $36.*

UNDERSEA CREATURES

Coki Beach Snorkeling. A good choice for novices who want to learn snorkeling (instruction and equipment usually are included) and see wildlife. *3 hrs. Cost: $25.*

Kayaking and Snorkeling Tour. Paddle on sit-atop kayaks through a marine sanctuary while a guide narrates both the on- and undersea scenes. *2½ hours. Cost: $50.*

Sailing and Snorkeling Tour. A romantic sail, a snorkeling lesson, and an attractive snorkeling site make this an excellent excursion. The boat may be a modern catamaran, a single-hull sailing yacht, or a sailing vessel done up to look like a pirate ship. *3 hrs. Cost: $47.*

Scuba Diving. This excursion to one or two choice sites via boat or off a beach may be limited to certified divers, may be open to novices who have been taking lessons on the ship, or may include instruction for beginners. *3 hrs. Cost: $40.*

Coming Ashore

Depending on how many ships are in port, cruise ships drop anchor in the harbor at Charlotte Amalie and tender passengers directly to the waterfront duty-free shops, dock at the Havensight Mall at the eastern end of the crescent-shaped bay, or dock at Crown Bay Marina a few miles west of town. The distance from Havensight to the duty-free shops is 3 km (1½ mi), which can be walked in less than half an hour, or a taxi can be hired for $2.50 per person, one-way. Tourist information offices are at the Havensight Mall (across from Bldg. No 1) for docking passengers and downtown near Ft. Christian (at the eastern end of the waterfront shopping area) for those coming ashore by tender. Both distribute free maps. From Crown Bay, it's also a half-hour walk or a $2.50 per person one-way cab ride.

In St. John, your ship may pause outside Cruz Bay Harbor to drop you off or drop anchor if it's spending the day. You'll be tendered to shore at the main town of Cruz Bay. The shopping district starts just across the street from the tender landing. You'll find an eclectic collection of shops, cozy restaurants, and places where you can just sit and take it all in. The island has few organized sites. Your best bet is to take a tour of the Virgin Islands National Park offered by your ship or independently with a taxi driver who will meet your tender. The drive takes you past luscious beaches to a restored sugar plantation.

Exploring St. Thomas

Numbers in the margin correspond to points of interest on the St. Thomas map.

CHARLOTTE AMALIE

❶ **Charlotte Amalie** is a hilly, overdeveloped shopping town. There are plenty of interesting historic sights here, and much of the town is quite pretty. So while you're shopping,

172

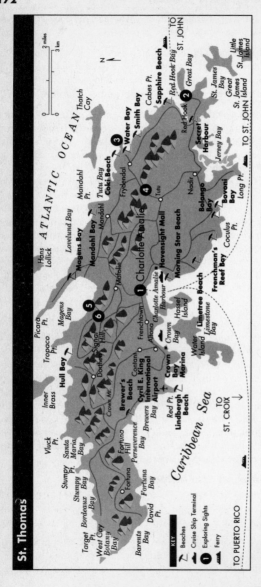

Charlotte Amalie, **1**
Coral World Marine
Park, **3**
Drake's Seat, **5**
Mountain Top, **6**

Red Hook, **2**
Tillett Gardens, **4**

take the time to see at least a few of the sights. For a great view of the town and the harbor, begin at the Spanish-style Hotel 1829, on Government Hill (also called Kongens Gade). A few yards farther up the road to the east is the base of the 99 Steps, a staircase "street" built by the Danes in the 1700s. Go up the steps (there are more than 99) and continue to the right to Blackbeard's Castle, originally Ft. Skytsborg. The massive five-story watchtower was built in 1679. It's now a dramatic perch from which to sip a drink, admire the harbor, and snap a photo of your ship.

Government House dates from 1867 and today contains the USVI governor's office. Inside are murals and paintings by Camille Pissarro. *Kongens Gade, tel. 340/774–0001. Open weekdays 8–5.*

Frederick Lutheran Church is the second-oldest Lutheran church in the hemisphere. Its walls date from 1793. *Norre Gade, tel. 340/776–1315. Open Mon.–Sat. 9–4.*

Emancipation Garden honors the 1848 freeing of the slaves and features a scaled-down model of the Liberty Bell. *Between Tolbod Gade and Ft. Christian.*

Ft. Christian protectively faces the harbor as St. Thomas's oldest standing structure (1672–80). The redbrick fortress has been used as a jail, governor's residence, town hall, courthouse, and church. A U.S. national landmark, the building houses a museum filled with historical artifacts. *Waterfront Hwy. just east of shopping district, tel. 340/776–4566. Open weekdays 8:30–4:30.*

The lime-green edifice on Kings Wharf is the **Legislature Building** (1874), seat of the 15-member USVI Senate since 1957. *Waterfront Hwy. across from Ft. Christian, tel. 340/774–0880. Open daily 8–5.*

THE SOUTH SHORE AND EAST END

2 Route 32 brings you into **Red Hook,** connected to the rest of the island only by dirt roads, which has grown from a sleepy little town into an increasingly self-sustaining village. At **American Yacht Harbor** you can stroll along the docks and visit with sailors and fishermen, stopping for a beer at Gunther's Spot or Tickles Dockside Pub.

❸ **Coral World Marine Park** has a three-level underwater observatory, the world's largest reef tank, and an aquarium with more than 20 TV-size tanks providing capsulized views of sea life. *Rte. 38, tel. 340/775–1555. Admission: $18. Open daily 9–5:30.*

❹ At **Tillett Gardens** on Route 38 (*see* Shopping, *below*), local artisans craft stained glass, pottery, and ceramics. Jim Tillett's paintings and fabrics are also on display.

NORTH SHORE/CENTER ISLANDS

❺ In the heights above Charlotte Amalie is **Drake's Seat,** the mountain lookout from which Sir Francis Drake was supposed to have kept watch over his fleet and looked for enemy ships of the Spanish fleet. Magens Bay and Mahogany Run are to the north, with the British Virgin Islands and Drake's Passage to the east. Off to the left, or west, are Fairchild Park, Mountain Top, Hull Bay, and smaller islands, such as the Inner and Outer Brass islands.

❻ West of Drake's Seat is **Mountain Top,** not only a tacky souvenir mecca, but also where the banana daiquiri was supposedly invented. There's a restaurant here and, at 1,500 ft above sea level, some spectacular views.

Exploring St. John
Cruz Bay doesn't have much in the way of sights. You'll mostly find shops, restaurants, and myriad opportunities to people-watch. A stroll along the waterfront will take you past the **Battery,** built on an 18th-century fortification. It's now the seat of the island's small government. You are welcome to wander around the grounds.

St. John's best sights are preserved in the sprawling **Virgin Islands National Park** (tel. 340/776–6201), which covers most of the island. Stunning vistas and beaches can be reached by taxi tour or car. If you have the day to spend, head for Cinnamon Bay. This National Park Service campground has a beach with water-sports equipment for rent, hiking, a modest restaurant, and cool showers.

Shopping
There are well over 400 shops in Charlotte Amalie alone, and near the Havensight docks there are at least 60 more, clustered in converted warehouses. Even die-hard shoppers

won't want to cover all the boutiques, since many peddle the same T-shirts and togs. Many visitors devote their shopping time on St. Thomas to the stores that sell handicrafts.

Although giveaway prices no longer abound, shoppers on St. Thomas can still save money. Today, a realistic appraisal puts prices on many items at about 20% off stateside prices, although liquor and perfume are often 50%–70% less expensive. What's more, there's no sales tax in the USVI, and you can take advantage of the $1,200-per-person duty-free allowance. Remember to save receipts.

Prices on luxury goods vary from shop to shop—if you find a good deal, take it. Prices on jewelry vary the most, and it's here that you'll still run across some real finds. Bargaining is not appreciated.

SHOPPING DISTRICTS

The major shopping area is Charlotte Amalie, in centuries-old buildings that once served as merchants' warehouses and that, for the most part, have been converted to retail establishments. Both sides of **Main Street** are lined with shops, as are the side streets and walkways between Main Street and the waterfront. These narrow lanes and arcades have names like Drake's Passage, Royal Dane Mall, Palm Passage, Trompeter Gade, Hibiscus Alley, and Raadet's Gade. **Back Street,** also called Vimmelskaft Gade (one block north of Main Street off Nye Gade) and streets adjacent to it—Garden Street, Kongens Gade, and Norre Gade—are also very good areas for browsing. At **Havensight Mall,** near the deep-water port, you'll find branches of downtown stores, as well as specialty shops and boutiques. Next door, there are additional shops at **Port of Sale.**

CHARLOTTE AMALIE

Unless otherwise noted, the following stores have branches both downtown and in Havensight Mall and are easy to find. If you have any trouble, shopping maps are available at the tourist offices and often from your ship's shore-excursion desk. U.S. citizens can carry back a gallon, or six "fifths," of liquor duty-free.

A. H. Riise Gift & Liquor Shops: Waterford, Wedgwood, Royal Crown, and Royal Doulton china; jewelry, pearls, and Rolex watches; liquors, cordials, and wines, including rare

St. John

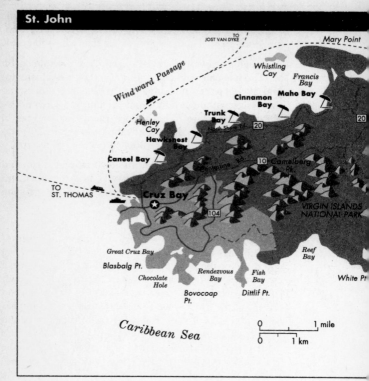

TO
JOST VAN DYKE

Mary Point

Windward Passage

Whistling Cay

Francis Bay

Cinnamon Bay

Maho Bay

Trunk Bay

North Shore Rd.

20

20

Henley Cay

Hawksnest Bay

Caneel Bay

Centerline Rd.

10 Camelberg Pk.

Cruz Bay

104

VIRGIN ISLANDS
NATIONAL PARK

TO
ST. THOMAS

Great Cruz Bay

Reef Bay

Blasbalg Pt.

Chocolate Hole

Rendezvous Bay

Fish Bay

White Pt

Bovocoap Pt.

Dittlif Pt.

Caribbean Sea

0   1 mile

0   1 km

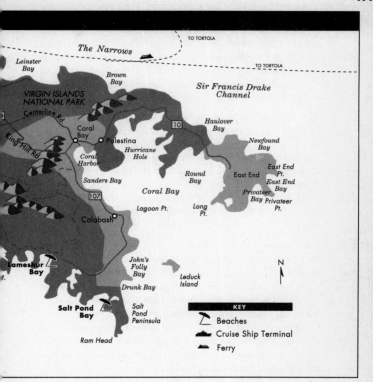

The Narrows

TO TORTOLA

TO TORTOLA

Leinster Bay

Brown Bay

Sir Francis Drake Channel

VIRGIN ISLANDS NATIONAL PARK

Centerline Rd.

Coral Bay

Palestina

Haulover Bay

10

Newfound Bay

King Hill Rd.

Coral Harbor

Hurricane Hole

East End Pt.

Round Bay

East End

East End Bay

Sanders Bay

107

Coral Bay

Privateer Bay

Privateer Pt.

Calabash

Lagoon Pt.

Long Pt.

Lameshur Bay

John's Folly Bay

Leduck Island

N

Drunk Bay

Salt Pond Bay

Salt Pond Peninsula

Ram Head

KEY

Beaches

Cruise Ship Terminal

Ferry

vintage cognacs; tobacco and imported cigars; fruits in brandy; barware from England; fragrances; and cosmetics. **Al Cohen's Discount Liquor** (Havensight Mall only): discount liquors. **Amsterdam Sauer:** one-of-a-kind fine jewelry. **Blue Carib Gems** (downtown only): jewelry of coral and Caribbean amber. **Boolchand's:** cameras, audio and video equipment.

The **Caribbean Marketplace** (Havensight Mall only): Caribbean handicrafts, including Caribelle batiks from St. Lucia; bikinis from the Cayman Islands; Sunny Caribee spices, soaps, teas, and coffees from Trinidad. **Down Island Traders** (downtown only): hand-painted calabash bowls; jams, jellies, spices, and herbs; herbal teas; high-mountain coffee from Jamaica; Caribbean handicrafts. The **English Shop** (Havensight only): china and crystal from Spode, Limoges, Royal Doulton, Portmeirion, and Noritaki.

The Gallery (in Down Island Traders, downtown): Haitian and local oil paintings, metal sculpture, wood carvings, painted screens and boxes, figures carved from stone, oversize papier-mâché figures. **Leather Shop:** Fendi, Bottega Veneta, other fine leather goods. **Little Switzerland:** Lalique, Baccarat, Waterford, and other crystal; Wedgwood, Royal Doulton, and other china. **Local Color** (downtown only): St. John artist Sloop Jones exhibits colorful, hand-painted island designs on cool dresses, T-shirts, and sweaters. **Native Arts and Crafts Cooperative:** (downtown only): handmade dolls, quilts, art, jewelry, jams, teas, and hot sauces.

Pampered Pirate (downtown only): Caribbean handicrafts, spices, sauces, jams, and Jamaican coffee. **Pusser's Close-Out Store** (Havensight Mall only): discounted nautically themed clothing. **Royal Caribbean** (no affiliation with the cruise line): audio-video equipment. **Tropicana Perfume Shoppes** (downtown only): fragrances.

TILLETT GARDENS

Tillett Gardens and Craft Complex (Estate Tutu, tel. 340/775– 1405) is more than worth the cab fare to reach it. The late Jim Tillett's artwork is on display, and you can watch craftsmen and artisans produce watercolors, silk-screened fabrics, pottery, enamel work, candles, and other handicrafts.

ST. JOHN

In St. John, the small shopping district runs from **Wharf-side Village** near the ferry landing to **Mongoose Junction**, just up the street from the cruise-ship dock and tender landing, with lots of shops tucked in between. **Colombian Emeralds** has two branches of its duty-free jewelry shops in St. John. Try either the main store at Mongoose Junction or its **Jewelers Warehouse** in Wharfside Village for emeralds, diamonds, and other jewels. For handcrafted jewelry try **Caravan Gallery. Pink Papaya** carries pottery, art, and gifts in bold Caribbean colors. Shop **Bamboula** and **Bougainvillea,** in Mongoose Junction, and **St. John Editions,** near the tender landing, for tropical clothing.

Sports

FISHING

Call **American Yacht Harbor** (tel. 340/775–6454), the **Charter Boat Center** (tel. 340/775–7990), or **Sapphire Beach Marina** (tel. 340/775–6100) all on the eastern end of St. Thomas, if you're interested in some serious angling.

GOLF

The Tom Fazio–designed **Mahogany Run Golf Course** (tel. 340/777–6006), north of Charlotte Amalie on St. Thomas, is a par-70, 18-hole course with a view of the BVI. The rate for 18 holes is $100, cart included.

WATER SPORTS

On St. Thomas, **Aqua Action** (tel. 340/775–6285) is a full-service, five-star shop that offers all levels of instruction at Secret Harbour Beach Resort. Another operator is the **Chris Sawyer Diving Center** (tel. 340/775–7320).

On St. John, **Cruz Bay Watersports** (tel. 340/776–6234) and **Low Key Watersports** (tel. 340/776–8999) provide snorkeling and scuba trips to nearby reefs.

Beaches

All beaches in the USVI are public, but occasionally you'll need to stroll through a resort to reach the sand. On St. Thomas, government-run **Magens Bay** is lively and popular because of its spectacular loop of white-sand beach, more than 1 km (½ mi) long, and its calm waters. Food, changing facilities, and rest rooms are available. **Coki Beach,** next to Coral World, offers great snorkeling among the reefs to the east and west of the beach. **Secret Harbour** is a pretty cove for superb snorkeling; go out to the left, near the rocks. **Morning Star Beach,** close to Charlotte Amalie, has a mostly sandy sea bottom with some rocks; snorkeling is good here when the current doesn't affect visibility. **Sapphire Beach** has a fine view of St. John and other islands. Snorkeling is excellent at the reef to the east, near Pettyklip Point. All kinds of water-sports gear can be rented, and dining facilities and rest rooms are at the adjacent resort.

Trunk Bay, in the Virgin Islands National Park, is the main beach on St. John, mostly because of its snorkeling trail. However, experienced snorkelers may find it tame and picked over, with too little coral or fish. Lifeguards are on duty and there are changing rooms, a snack bar, and picnic tables. **Hawksnest Beach** is closer and less used, but doesn't have showers. **Cinnamon Bay** has it all—a great beach, showers, water-sports equipment, and a snack bar.

Dining
Some restaurants add a 10%–15% service charge.

ST. THOMAS

$–$$ **Beni Iguana's.** Here sushi is served as "edible art" in a charming Danish courtyard. A pictorial menu makes ordering by the piece, plate, or platter much easier. *Grand Hotel Court, tel. 340/777–8744. No credit cards. Closed Sun.*

$ **Gladys' Cafe.** With a welcoming smile, owner Gladys Isles will tempt you to try local favorites, such as whole pan-fried fish topped with a tangy creole sauce, conch simmered with butter and onions, or chunks of Caribbean lobster served sandwich-style. For the less adventurous, the grilled chicken salad is a winner, too. *Royal Dane Mall, tel. 340/774–6604. AE. No dinner.*

$ **Zorba's Sagapo.** Greek dishes, like salads and Mediterranean-style seafood, are the specialties at this converted 19th-century residence. You can munch on fresh bread while looking out over the harbor. *Government Hill near Hotel 1829, Charlotte Amalie, tel. 340/776–0444. AE, MC, V.*

ST. JOHN

$$ **Global Village Cuisine at Latitude 18.** Choose either the cozy but open-air dining room or the breezy bar-dining area. Hamburgers, sandwiches, and salads make up the lunch menu. *Mongoose Junction, tel. 340/693–8677. AE, MC, V.*

$$ Lime Inn. This open-air restaurant attracts mainland transplants who call St. John home and visitors who come for the congenial atmosphere as well as quiche, pasta, and sandwiches. *Downtown Cruz Bay, tel. 340/776–6425. AE, MC, V. Closed Sun.*

$$ Sun Dog Cafe. Tucked under umbrellas at the upper reaches of Mongoose Junction, this nifty spot offers eclectic fare. The menu includes barbecue pork, cheese and veggies in phyllo dough, hot dogs, and great smoothies. *Mongoose Junction, tel. 340/693–8340. No credit cards.*

San Juan, Puerto Rico

Although Puerto Rico is part of the United States, few cities in the Caribbean are as steeped in Spanish tradition as San Juan. Within a seven-block neighborhood in Old San Juan are restored 16th-century buildings, museums, art galleries, bookstores, 200-year-old houses with balustraded balconies overlooking narrow, cobblestone streets. In contrast, San Juan's sophisticated Condado and Isla Verde areas have glittering hotels, flashy Las Vegas-style shows, casinos, and discos. Out in the countryside is the 28,000-acre El Yunque rain forest, with more than 240 species of trees growing at least 100 ft high. You can stretch your sea legs on dramatic mountain ranges, numerous trails, vast caves, coffee plantations, old sugar mills, and hundreds of beaches. No wonder San Juan is one of the busiest ports of call in the Caribbean.

Like any other big city, San Juan has its share of crime. Guard your wallet or purse, and avoid walking in the area between Old San Juan and the Condado.

Currency
The U.S. dollar is the official currency of Puerto Rico.

Telephones
Calling the United States from Puerto Rico is the same as calling within the states. Local calls from a public phone cost 25¢ for every five minutes. You can use the long-distance telephone service office in the cruise-ship terminal. You'll find a phone center by the Paseo de la Princesa.

Shore Excursions

The following are good choices in San Juan. They may not be offered by all cruise lines. Times and prices are approximate.

LOCAL FLAVORS

Bacardi Rum Distillery. After seeing how it is made, you can sample and buy some Bacardi rum. *2 hrs. Cost: $20.*

San Juan Nightlife Tour. Several major hotels (like the Condado Plaza) have very exciting revues, especially those that feature flamenco or Latin dancers. Admission includes a drink or two. *1– 2½ hrs. Cost: $34–$40.*

NATURAL BEAUTY

El Yunque Rain Forest. A 45-minute drive heads east to the Caribbean National Forest, where you can walk along various trails, see waterfalls, and climb the observation tower. Lunch at a country restaurant is included. *4½ hrs. Cost: $48.*

Coming Ashore

Cruise ships dock within a couple of blocks of Old San Juan. The Paseo de la Princesa, a tree-lined promenade beneath the city wall, is a nice place for a stroll—you can admire the local crafts and stop at the refreshment kiosks. A tourist information booth is in the cruise-terminal area. Major sights in the Old San Juan area are mere blocks from the piers, but be aware that the streets are narrow and steeply inclined in places. A ride to anywhere else in the Old San Juan area costs $6; a 10- or 15-minute taxi ride to the Condado, Ocean Park, or Miramar costs $10.

To get to Cataño and the Bacardi Rum Plant, take the 50¢ ferry that leaves from the cruise piers every half hour. Your best bet, other than an organized ship excursion, to reach Bayamón and Caparra (still within the San Juan Metro area) is to take a taxi. Taxis line up to meet ships. Metered cabs authorized by the Public Service Commission charge an initial $1; after that, it's about 10¢ for each additional ⅓ mi. Insist that the meter be turned on, and pay only what is shown, plus a tip of 10%–15%. You can negotiate with taxi drivers for specific trips, and you can hire a taxi for as little as $20 per hour for sightseeing tours.

If your feet fail you in Old San Juan, climb aboard the free open-air trolleys that rumble through the narrow streets. Take one from the docks or board anywhere along the route.

Exploring San Juan

Numbers in the margin correspond to points of interest on the Old San Juan map.

OLD SAN JUAN

Old San Juan, the original city founded in 1521, contains authentic and carefully preserved examples of 16th- and 17th-century Spanish colonial architecture. Graceful wrought-iron balconies decorated with lush green hanging plants extend over narrow, cobblestone streets. Seventeenth-century walls still partially enclose the old city. Designated a U.S. National Historic Zone in 1950, Old San Juan is packed with shops, open-air cafés, private homes, tree-shaded squares, monuments, plaques, pigeons, people, and traffic jams. It's faster to walk than to take a cab. Nightlife is quiet, even spooky during the low season; you'll find more to do in New San Juan, especially the Condado area.

① **San Cristóbal,** the 18th-century fortress that guarded the city from land attacks, is known as the Gibraltar of the West Indies. San Cristóbal is larger than El Morro (*see below*), and has spectacular views of the city. *Calle Norzagaray, tel. 787/729–6960. Admission $2. Open daily 9–5.*

② The **Plaza de Armas** is the original main square of Old San Juan. In the plaza is a fountain with statues representing the four seasons.

③ West of the main square stands **La Intendencia,** a handsome, three-story neoclassical building that was home to the Spanish Treasury from 1851 to 1898. Today it houses Puerto Rico's State Department. *Calle San José at Calle San Francisco, tel. 787/722–2121, ext. 230. Admission free. Open weekdays 8–noon and 1–4:30.*

④ On the north side of the Plaza de Armas is San Juan's city hall, the **Alcaldía.** Built between 1604 and 1789, it was fashioned after Madrid's city hall, with arcades, balconies, and a courtyard. An art gallery is on the first floor. *Tel. 787/724–7171, ext. 2391. Open weekdays 8–4.*

Old San Juan

ATLANTIC OCEAN

N

TO THE CONDADO

Norzagaray

San Sebastián

Las Monjas

Sol
Luna
O'Donnel

San Francisco
Sansta
Fortaleza

Ponce de Léon

Muñoz Rivera

Calle Recinto
Oeste

Tetuán
Recinto Sur

Paseo de
Marina

Del Muelle

*Bahía de
San Juan*

Paseo de
la Princesa
Arsenal

0   550 yards
0   500 meters

Alcaldía, **4**
Catedral San
Juan, **5**
Convento
de los
Dominicos, **8**
La Fortaleza, **9**

Fuerte San
Felipe del
Morro, **10**
Iglesia de San
Jose, **7**
La
Intendencia, **3**

Museo Pablo
Casals, **6**
Plaza de
Armas, **2**
San
Cristóbal, **1**

The remains of Ponce de León are in a marble tomb in the ❺ **Catedral de San Juan** on Calle Cristo. This great Catholic shrine had humble beginnings in the early 1520s as a thatch-top wood structure that was destroyed by a hurricane. It was reconstructed in 1540, when the graceful circular staircase and vaulted ceilings were added, but most of the work was done in the 19th century. *153 Calle Cristo, tel. 787/722–0861. Admission free. Open daily 8:30–4.*

❻ The **Museo Pablo Casals** exhibits memorabilia of the famed Spanish cellist, who made his home in Puerto Rico for the last 20 years of his life. *101 Calle San Sebastián, Plaza de San José, tel. 787/723–9185. Admission: $1. Open Tues.– Sat. 9:30- -5:30.*

❼ In the center of Plaza San José is the **Iglesia de San José.** With its series of vaulted ceilings, it is a fine example of 16th-century Spanish Gothic architecture. *Calle San Sebastián, tel. 787/725–7501. Admission free. Open Mon.–Sat. 8:30– 4; mass Sun. at 12:15.*

❽ Next door to the Iglesia de San José is the 16th-century **Convento de los Dominicos,** which houses an ornate 18th- century altar, religious manuscripts, artifacts, and art. *98 Calle Norzagaray, tel. 787/721–6866. Admission free. Chapel museum open Mon.–Sat. 9–5.*

❾ **La Fortaleza,** the Western Hemisphere's oldest executive mansion in continuous use, overlooks the harbor from a hilltop. Built originally in the 1500s as a fortress, it has been dressed up over the centuries with marble and mahogany, medieval towers, and stained-glass galleries. Guided tours are every hour on the hour in English, on the half hour in Spanish. *Calle Recinto Oeste, tel. 787/721–7000, ext. 2211. Admission free. Open weekdays 9–4.*

❿ San Juan's most famous sight is undoubtedly **Fuerte San Felipe del Morro,** known as El Morro, set on a rocky promontory on the northwestern tip of the old city. Rising 140 ft above the sea, the massive, six-level Spanish fortress is a labyrinth of dungeons, ramps, turrets, and tunnels. Built to protect the port, El Morro has a commanding view of the harbor and Old San Juan. Its small museum traces the history of the fortress. *Calle Norzagaray, tel. 787/729– 6960. Admission $2. Open daily 9–5.*

NEW SAN JUAN

In **Puerta de Tierra,** 1 km (½ mi) east of the pier, is Puerto Rico's white-marble capitol, dating from the 1920s. Another kilometer east, at the tip of Puerta de Tierra, tiny Ft. San Jeronimo perches over the Atlantic like an afterthought. Added to San Juan's fortifications in the late 18th century, the structure barely survived the British attack of 1797.

Santurce, the district between Miramar on the west and the Laguna San José on the east, is a busy mixture of shops, markets, and offices. The classically designed Universidad del Sagrado Corazón (Sacred Heart University) is home of the Museo Contemporáneo del Arte de Puerto Rico (Museum of Contemporary Puerto Rican Art) (Barat Bldg., tel. 787/268–0049).

SAN JUAN ENVIRONS

The **Bacardi Rum Plant,** along the bay, conducts 45-minute tours of the bottling plant, museum, and distillery, which can produce 100,000 gallons of rum a day—yes, you'll be offered a sample. A ferry to Cataño departs from next to the cruise-ship docks every half hour from 6 AM until 10 PM, at a cost of 50¢. *Rte. 888, Km 2.6, Cataño, tel. 787/788–1500. Admission free. Tours every 30 min, Mon.–Sat. 9–10:30 and noon–4; closed holidays.*

Along Route 5 from Cataño to Bayamón, you'll find the **Barrilito Rum Plant.** The grounds include a 200-year-old plantation home and a 150-year-old windmill, which is listed in the National Register of Historic Places. *Rte. 5, Km 1.6, Bayamón, tel. 787/785–3490. Admission free. Open weekdays 8–11:30 and 1–4:30.*

About 6 km (4 mi) from San Juan on Route 2 West, you'll find the **Caparra Ruins,** where, in 1508, Ponce de León established the island's first settlement. Within the fort ruins is the small Museum of the Conquest and Colonization of Puerto Rico and its historic documents, exhibits, and excavated artifacts. *Rte. 2, Km 6.6, tel. 787/781–4795. Admission free. Open Tues.–Sat. 8:30–4:30.*

Past the Caparra Ruins, Route 2 brings you to **Bayamón,** about 11 km (7 mi) from central San Juan. In the Central Park, across from the city hall, are some historic buildings and a 1934 sugarcane train that runs through the park.

Shopping

San Juan is not a free port, and you won't find bargains on electronics and perfumes. However, shopping for native crafts can be fun. Popular souvenirs and gifts include *santos* (small, hand-carved figures of saints or religious scenes), hand-rolled cigars, handmade lace, carnival masks, Puerto Rican rum, and fancy men's shirts called *guayaberas*.

Old San Juan is filled with shops, especially on **Cristo, La Fortaleza,** and **San Francisco** streets. You can get discounts on Hathaway shirts and clothing by Christian Dior and Ralph Lauren at **Hathaway Factory Outlet** (203 Calle Cristo, tel. 787/723–8946) and on raincoats at the **London Fog Factory Outlet** (156 Calle Cristo, tel. 787/722–4334). For one-of-a-kind local crafts, head for **Puerto Rican Arts & Crafts** (204 Calle Fortaleza, tel. 787/725–5596) or the **Haitian Gallery** (367 Calle Fortaleza, tel. 787/725–0986).

Sports

GOLF

There are four Robert Trent Jones–designed 18-hole courses shared by the **Hyatt Dorado Beach Hotel** and the **Hyatt Regency Cerromar Beach Hotel** (Rte. 693, Dorado, tel. 787/796–1234, ext. 3238 or 3016). You'll also find 18-hole courses at **Wyndham Palmas del Mar Resort** (Rte. 906, Humacao, tel. 787/852–6000), **Westin Río Mar Resort and Country Club** (6000 Río Mar Blvd., Río Grande, tel. 787/888–6000), and **Bahia Beach Plantation** (Rte. 187, Río Grande, tel. 787/256–5600).

HIKING

Dozens of trails lace **El Yunque.** Information is available at the El Portal Tropical Forest Center (Rte. 191, tel. 787/888–1810). Admission is $3.

WATER SPORTS

Virtually all the resort hotels on San Juan's Isla Verde (*see* Beaches, *below*) rent small craft.

Beaches

By law, all of Puerto Rico's beaches are open to the public (except for the Caribe Hilton's artificial beach in San Juan). The government runs 13 public *balnearios* (beaches), which have lockers, showers, and picnic tables; some have playgrounds. *Admission free; parking $2. Open daily 8–5 in summer, Tues.–Sun. 9–6 rest of the year.*

Isla Verde is a white sandy beach close to metropolitan San Juan. Backed by several resorts, the beach offers picnic tables and good snorkeling, with equipment rentals nearby.

Dining

Tips are expected, and appreciated, by restaurant waitstaff (15%–18% if a service charge isn't included).

$$–$$$ **La Mallorquina.** The food here is basic Puerto Rican and Spanish fare, but the atmosphere is what recommends the spot. Said to date from 1848, this is the oldest restaurant in Puerto Rico, with pale pink walls and whirring ceiling fans, and a nattily attired and friendly waitstaff. *207 Calle San Justo, tel. 787/722–3261. AE, MC, V. Closed Sun.*

$–$$ **Amadeus.** In an atmosphere of gentrified Old San Juan, a trendy, pretty crowd enjoys a nouvelle Caribbean menu. The roster of appetizers includes plantain mousse with shrimp; sample entrées range from Cajun-grilled mahimahi to chicken and steak sandwiches. *106 Calle San Sebastián, tel.787/722–8635. AE, MC, V.*

Nightlife

Almost every ship stays in San Juan late or even overnight to give passengers an opportunity to revel in the nightlife—the most sophisticated in the Caribbean.

CASINOS

By law, all casinos are in hotels. Alcoholic drinks are not permitted at the gaming tables, although free soft drinks, coffee, and sandwiches are available. The atmosphere is quite refined, and many patrons dress to the nines, but informal attire is usually fine. Casinos set their own hours, which change seasonally, but generally operate from noon to 4 AM. Casinos are in the following hotels: **Condado Plaza Hotel, Carib Inn, El San Juan, Ramada, San Juan Marriott,** and **San Juan Grand.**

DANCE AND MUSIC CLUBS

In Old San Juan, young people flock to **Club Lazer** (251 Calle Cruz, tel. 787/725–7581). In Puerta de Tierra, Condado, and Isla Verde, the thirtysomething crowd heads for

Amadeus (El San Juan Hotel, tel. 787/791–1000), **Café Matisse** (Av. Ashford, Condado, tel. 787/723–7910), and **Egipto the Club** (Av. Robert Todd, Santurce, tel. 787/725–4664 or 787/725–4675) for live music and dancing.

Ports of Embarkation and Disembarkation

Miami

The Port of Miami is on Dodge Island, across from the downtown area via a five-lane bridge. Just before the bridge on the mainland is the large and attractive Bayside Marketplace, whose waterfront ambience, two stories of shops and restaurants, and street entertainers provide a pleasant alternative to the cruise terminals if you arrive before boarding begins.

LONG-TERM PARKING

Street-level lots are right in front of the cruise terminals. Just leave your luggage with a porter, tip him, and park. The cost is $8 per day.

Port Canaveral

Florida's Port Canaveral is used primarily by ships that combine their sailings with a pre- or post-cruise package at an Orlando theme park. Walt Disney World, Magic Kingdom, Disney–MGM Studios, Epcot Center, Universal Studios, and Sea World are about an hour by car. The Kennedy Space Center is 15 mi (24 km) away and Cocoa Beach is nearby.

LONG-TERM PARKING

An outdoor long-term parking lot is directly outside the terminal and costs about $7 per day.

FROM THE AIRPORT

The Orlando airport is 45 minutes away from the docks. Taxi rates are very expensive, so try taking the $20-per-person **Cocoa Beach Shuttle** (tel. 800/633–0427) bus instead, but call first to make a reservation.

San Juan

Puerto Rico's capital has become a major port of embarkation for cruises to the "deep" or southern Caribbean.

FROM THE AIRPORT

The ride from the **Luis Muñoz Marín International Airport,** east of downtown San Juan, to the docks in Old San Juan takes about 20 minutes. The white "taxi turistico" cabs, marked by a logo on the door, have a fixed rate of $16 to the piers; there is a small fee for luggage. Other taxi companies charge by the mile, which can cost a little more. Be sure the taxi driver starts the meter, or agree on a fare beforehand.

INDEX

NOTES

NOTES

NOTES

NOTES

NOTES

NOTES

Looking for a different kind of vacation?

Fodor's makes it easy with a full line of specialty guidebooks to suit a variety of interests—from adventure to romance to language help.

Fodor's. For the world of ways you travel.